GRATEFULLY YOURS,
FROM NAZI UNTERMENSCH
TO A PATCH
IN THE ROSE GARDEN

Gratefully Yours, From Nazi Untermensch to a Patch in the Rose Garden

A Historic Memoir

Rita Steinhardt Botwinick, PhD

\<teneo\> //press
AMHERST, NEW YORK

Requests for permission should be directed to
permissions@tenepress.com, or mailed to:
Teneo Press
100 Corporate Parkway Suite 128
Amherst, NY 14226

Library of Congress Cataloging-in-Publication Data

Steinhardt Botwinick, Rita
Gratefully Yours, From Nazi Untermensch to a Patch in the
Rose Garden: A Historical Memoir / Rita Steinhardt Botwinick
p. cm.
ISBN 978-1-934844-56-4 (alk. paper)

Writing a memoir reopens old wounds. I had completed a draft of this book and was ready to put it aside; it was just too painful. But, when my Brandeis book group decided to make Gratefully Yours their reading assignment, their enthusiastic encouragement sent me back to the computer. I salute and thank them.

TABLE OF CONTENTS

List of Photos

Gratefully Yours,
From Nazi Untermensch
to a Patch
in the Rose Garden

Introduction

To escape the Florida heat, my husband Leonard and I rented a cottage one summer in Hendersonville, North Carolina. A nearby music school offered frequent concerts to the public, directed by talented staff and performed by outstanding students. We attended often and one such occasion is etched into my memory. The auditorium, an open shell, was set in a forest of old pines. It had rained earlier and now the afternoon sun was reflected in countless droplets glistening on the branches while a lazy breeze sweetened the air with the aroma of the trees. As the maestro lifted his baton I whispered to Len: "I think I've been transported into a fairy land." He put his lips near my ear and said: "The little girl from Winzig has come a long way." How true. With a sigh of contentment I replied, "Thank you, America."

Gratitude to this country is the central impetus to the writing of this memoir. America not only allowed me to live, it helped me to thrive. Of course, this nation has many problems, but I believe Uncle Sam, despite his warts, remains sound of mind and vigorous of body. Our founding fathers made us the fortunate beneficiary of a durable Constitution that has allowed this country to endure great ordeals, to be balanced in times of prosperity, yet to be flexible enough to adjust to the challenges of our fast-changing world. As ever, nostalgic views of the past prompt doubts, concerns, and complaints, but surely our descendants will look back at this century with equally unrealistic wistfulness.

My life experience tells me this is still the land of opportunities. Our laws do not bar any citizens from achieving realistic goals. The emphasis is on *realistic*. It is unkind and untrue to tell children their dreams—or perhaps their parents' hopes—can be realized if they just try hard enough. Not all things are possible; some goals are beyond our best efforts. There are physical, intellectual, and emotional hurdles that cannot be cleared, and the height of the bar may have to be adjusted. Fifty years in the front of classrooms has taught me that.

My metamorphosis from unwanted outcast under the swastika to confident teacher in America was made possible by helping hands that reached out to me. I was nine years old when Hitler came to power in 1933. For the next six years, I was treated as a source of dangerous contamination of the German people. Three years after the proclamation of the Third Reich, I was declared unfit to share a classroom with former schoolmates. I left home to attend schools maintained by the Jewish community in the Silesian capital of city of Breslau. But that refuge was short-lived; by Nazi decree all such institutions of learning and training were closed down after the Crystal Night Pogrom on November 9, 1938. For more than two years, I had no academic training at all. When we escaped to the United States in December 1939, I feared American schools might reject me. If I were admitted, would I be placed with much younger students? In addition to the gaps in my education, my knowledge of English was about equal to that of a three-year-old. To my great relief, I was welcomed into the school system of the State of New York. Within two years, I was the proud recipient of a Regents high school diploma. My teachers urged me to go to college. Although we had no money, my parents supported my hope to continue my education. Was it possible? Yes! There were scholarships and work programs and the University of South Carolina offered me both. I took the train to Columbia with a mixture of anticipation and apprehension. Three years later, I had acquired a Southern accent, a college degree, and, to my intense joy, a group of friends. What an exhilarating experience to be accepted, even cherished by my peers.

My unsmiling face in my German passport has an uncanny resemblance to a picture of Anne Frank. I read her *Diary* many times and mourned her fate as if she were a family member. For many years I wondered: Why did America's golden door open for me and not for her? Eventually, I accepted the fact that there is no answer to that question. Nonetheless, my visceral connection to Anne may have motivated my continuing immersion in Holocaust history. For half a century, I read, taught, and wrote on the Shoah. I believe those studies influenced a second resolve for the writing of this memoir.

Before we crossed the Atlantic Ocean to the United States, my family lived in a small town in Germany named Winzig, then located in the province of Silesia in southeastern Prussia. Although literature on the Hitler era is vast, only a few books deal with Jewish persecution in the hinterland, in the small communities where everyone knew everyone else. Yes, all Jewish people, wherever they resided, were subjected to intimidation, lost their German citizenship, were denied the right to work, were robbed of their assets, were publicly declared the most dangerous enemy of the German people, and finally were likened to vermin to be annihilated. During the years before Auschwitz, though, before implementation of the Nazis' "final solution of the Jewish question," rural Jews suffered a more intense persecution due to their isolation. As Christian friends deserted them, some willingly, some reluctantly, the Jewish disconnect from the outside world was nearly absolute. In cities, Jewish families, even after they were segregated from the Aryan population, continued to have the solace of companionship. Crowded into smaller and smaller quarters, without privacy, their scant ration cards marked with the capital J, deprived of fresh and wholesome food, dreading an uncertain future, they nonetheless had consolation in each other's company. Until trains to camps in the east ended German Jewish existence, these city Jews maintained social connections with friends and relatives. Barred from the use of telephones, radios, and public transport, subjected to curfews, city Jews and their elected leaders nevertheless established and maintained many essential services, including a number of cultural activities. Jewish schools, forbidden by Nazi authorities, were maintained in secret and provided boys and girls with a much-needed routine. Their hours of attendance, homework, and friendships provided some sense of normalcy. Adults, too, found various activities that approached the illusion of time well spent. Jewish musicians and lecturers volunteered time and talent to inform and entertain, rabbis and cantors held religious services. Until the very end, self-help organizations attempted to feed and clothe the poorest among them; doctors and dentists tried to comfort the ailing, while lawyers and former civil service employees guided hopeful emigrants through the morass of paperwork. Survivors still recall card games, the pleasure of exchanging books. Blond, blue-eyed Jews might risk a trip to visit forbidden venues, such as shops, parks, even concerts. Petty quarrels could not diminish the outpouring of affection, commiseration, and need for each other.

Such support did not exist for isolated, rural families. The absence of anonymity frightened even the most well-meaning gentile neighbor from visiting Jewish friends, lest it cost the neighbor his or her own freedom. There were *Spitzels* (Nazi informers) everywhere and it was dangerous to oppose, even to appear to oppose, the Nazis by word or deed. The following chapters offer a glimpse into the rural corner of pre-Holocaust Jewish families.

Though I would be pleased to make a contribution to the history of the Shoah, the essence this memoir is my expression of gratitude for the blessings of America, for acceptance, for work, and for the opportunity to rear children. The story of the Steinhardts is unique only in its details, it has been lived by millions whose lives echo and affirm the spirit of the Statue of Liberty and the sonnet by Emma Lazarus engraved at the base of the Lady with the Lamp:

"...give me your tired, your poor,

Your huddled masses yearning to breathe free,

The wretched refuse of your teeming shore.

Send these, the homeless, tempest-tossed to me,

I lift my lamp beside the golden door."

(from *The New Colossus*, 1883)

Chapter 1

Changes Come to Winzig

An unfamiliar noise woke me up. I went into the adjoining room, but my parents were not in their bed. Then, I saw three silhouettes standing in front of the window. Why, I wondered, were my mother, father, and oldest brother Walter, all in their night clothing, looking down into the yard below? And what were these strange grunts and thumps, a scream, followed by colorful curses in an almost-unintelligible Silesian dialect? I tugged on Walter's pajama pants and he stepped over to make room for me. Eight years older than I, he was ever my protector, teacher, and defender. I was the youngest of four children and the only girl, and I often needed Walter's sympathetic understanding. The children born between us, brothers Dicker and Friedel, had no patience with the little sister who tried to tag along with them and their friends.

Walter said, "Take a look, *Schwesterchen*, (little sister), Winzig's version of a revolution. Your first, but I don't think your last."

My mother questioned the appropriateness of allowing a nine-year-old girl to witness this ugly spectacle: below the window men were pounding each other with fists and clubs. But she did not send me away and I was surprised and pleased.

"A revolution? In Winzig? In our yard?"

Walter explained to me that the brawl had nothing to do with our family. This fight was political, he said, a prelude to the scheduled elections. Members of one of the relatively new party, the National Socialist German Workers' Party—everyone called them Nazis—were instigating fights with members of other political factions. I turned to my brother.

"But why are they hitting each other?"

"To influence the coming election."

I still did not understand how rolling around in the dirt and hurting one another could help a candidate running for office. Walter, always my mentor, explained this tactic was called intimidation. Still confused, I shook my head.

"Are you scared?" asked my father as he reached for my hand.

"Oh, no, Papa." I felt perfectly safe in the presence of the two most important men in my life.

We stared out the window as the political battle continued.

"Are the Nazis fighting the Communists?" I asked. My teachers had warned us about the terrible danger of the Red Menace.

My father pursed his lips and shook his head.

"No Communists in Winzig," he said. "Well, maybe one man, but only when he's drunk. In the big cities, Nazis and Communists battle it out, but not here. Can you see the ones in the brown shirts? They are the troublemakers, the instigators. Thank God, their man, his name is Hitler, doesn't have a chance to win."

"Rabble," mother added, but Walter said, "Don't be too hard on them, *Mutti* (Dear Mother). Most of these fellows would rather work than brawl. I recognize several them; they dropped out of school on their sixteenth birthdays. But they can't find work and their social security checks are gone by mid-week. So, they do anything to earn a little money, like shouting '*Heil Hitler*' and picking fights. I doubt they know much or care much about Hitler's ideas for the country."

He pointed at some of the figures in the yard.

"See the men in gray shirts? Not exactly in uniform, but they like to dress in the leftovers from the Great War. Most of them are veterans and they belong to an organization called the *Stahlhelm* (Steel Helmets). Their choice for president is to reelect an old army general named Paul von Hindenburg. As long as they oppose the Nazis, Hitler won't win."

The scuffle moved across the street to the blacksmith's corner, and we returned to our beds. In the morning, my mother asked Lena, our maid, to scrub down the stone steps, as they were stained with blood. The gossips who gathered around the public water pumps reported no one had been seriously hurt in the fracas, just cuts and bruises. Who won? The melee had been too confused to produce a victor.

This was my introduction to the beginning of the end of Germany's Weimar Republic. In Berlin, Hamburg, Munich, and other cities, pre-election clashes, most often between Nazis and Communists, often became serious. But we lived in the hinterland where Prussian conservatism still dominated. Even in 1932, the owners of large estates controlled much of the rural economic, political, and social life. Although their land holdings had shrunk over the centuries, the "von" before their surnames awarded them automatic respect and deference. Serfdom was long gone and small and mid-sized farms had been carved from some of their land; nonetheless their influence over the untitled, the commoners, still claimed our awe.

The First World War had disrupted much of the old social order, but the changes wrung from Germany's defeat were more obvious in the cities. Life in the country was slower to reject the past. Most rural people still yearned for the defunct monarchy, and spoke reverently of the days when orderliness and obedience kept society marching in traditional step. Parents took pride in their compliant and respectful children, but worried about their willful or ambitious ones. Church and school applauded good behavior rather than curiosity and intellect. Rural women shared none of the freedoms of their emancipated sisters in the cities. These country women worked from sun-up to sun-down, looking old and worn out at forty. Social standing was determined by thrift, modesty, adherence to conventional morality, and knowing one's proper place on the social ladder.

Here, the heavy hand of tradition continued to determine questions of inheritance. The Weimar Constitution stipulated no legal barriers to the right of parents to leave their property as they wished, but ancient customs did not change. Although a younger son might be more suited to run the farm, the oldest still inherited the land and all it entailed: house, barns, animals, equipment, everything. The fear remained deep-rooted that dividing the property would soon reduce it to the size of garden plots. Only if the oldest child was a girl could a younger son claim the inheritance. But what of other sons? The aristocracy had solved the problem by encouraging them to join the officer corps of the army, seek appointments in government ministries, or secure positions in the Lutheran church. Such careers were almost exclusively reserved for the gentry, and rarely available to members of the middle and lower classes.

There were options, though. Some of the common-born younger brothers might be apprenticed to craftsmen or go to the cities and join the growing class of industrial workers. Farmers' daughters could expect a suitable dowry upon marriage. But many, perhaps most, of the younger brothers remained at home. They settled for the life of underpaid laborers for the heir, the oldest brother. They might live in an attic room. They milked and plowed, weeded and cleaned. They ate with the family but would not expect the best part of the chicken on their plates. A good suit hung in their wardrobe, donned mostly for church or funerals. The kitchen stove kept them warm on cold winter evenings and they might join friends for a beer on Saturday nights. They had no reasonable expectation to marry girls from well-to-do families. Although they owned no land, they usually voted for conservative parties. Like their fathers, they mistrusted the Socialists, and had little use for the Nazis whose leader sprang from the lower middle class, just one generation away from poverty. As good Lutherans, they would not vote for the Catholic Center Party, which shared with the Socialists the governments during the fourteen years of the existence of the Weimar Republic.

Winzig's neediest were the agricultural day laborers. They earned wages in spring, summer, and during the fall harvest season, but found little employment in winter. My mother once asked me to the take some outgrown clothes to such a family. I still remember my dread when the grateful mother offered me a treat: a slice of bread dipped into sugar beet syrup. I thanked her and said I would eat it later. Actually, I was shocked at such destitution: unpainted walls, floors of packed dirt, wet rags used as diapers hanging around the stove, the windows black with flies, and a choking, indefinable stench. Hitler found some supporters among these families. They had nothing to lose and the Nazis promised work and equality of opportunity for all. While many of the city poor joined the Communist Party after the economic disaster of the Great Depression, some of their rural counterparts were attracted to Hitler's National Socialism.

Winzig, the place we all called home, had operated this way for centuries. The town received its charter in 1285. The medieval walls had crumbled long ago, but the center of town remained the hub of civic life. City hall stood in the middle of the main square, paradoxically called the Ring; four major streets emptied from the corners. Stores and offices lined the Ring; it was the best business address. Some of the narrow-fronted buildings were two or three stories high, as business was conducted on the ground floor with living quarters above. Outside the Ring were the homes of farmers and their service shops such as blacksmiths and wheelwrights. The farm houses facing the street looked deceptively neat and trim. Their back yards, however, were a jumble of barns, equipment, outhouses, sheds, chicken coops, wandering poultry, and, inevitably, a grand pile of manure. Unlike their American counterparts, most European farmers did not reside on their fields; experiences of centuries of warfare clustered them near the walled towns or manor houses, places to which they could escape the next battle.

A Prussian garrison had been stationed in Winzig between 1743 and 1871. That military presence, however, was not enough to promote the town's growth. Lack of a reliable source of water precluded its participation in the country's industrialization. The number of its inhabitants remained small and fairly static; between 1930 and 1940 they totaled about 2,200. Winzig survived for 800 years because its residents provided necessary services for surrounding villages, their inhabitants approximated 10,000.

On weekdays, a trickle of horse-drawn wagons rumbled into town, but their influx swelled to a steady flow on Saturdays. Families from neighboring communities, dressed in their second-best (their best was reserved for church, weddings, or funerals), came to do business. They might shop for food not grown in their gardens, call on a shoemaker, consider a purchase in one of the clothing stores, retain the farrier to shoe a horse, see to the repair of a wagon wheel, consult with a carpenter, hire a roofer, or call upon the grain mill. Special occasions required a visit to the photographer's studio for a formal portrait, father standing, mother sitting, boys and girls lined up according to age. An engagement could prompt a call at the jewelry store, and only dire need could persuade the ailing to seek out the doctor or the dentist. Legal problems brought clients to the lawyer and financial business might prompt a hesitant knock on the banker's door. By afternoon, after a brief respite at one of the local beer gardens, families headed home in time to care for their waiting animals.

Winzig was nestled atop a hill that dominated the countryside. Its two church steeples, the Lutheran one some meters higher than its Catholic counterpart, were visible for many miles in all directions. The town's wide streets were lined by a profusion of trees, especially oaks and chestnuts. Visitors claimed to envy our invigorating air and lack of factories, but they did not share our long, cold winters, nor did they realize the quantity and quality of entertainment was meager by city standards. A few sports clubs, church choirs, several bars, a monthly movie shown in a hired hall —that was all. Residents who wanted to see a play, attend an opera, hear a concert, visit a museum, or buy stylish clothes had to travel to a city. My mother's choice was Berlin or Breslau and my father understood— although he did not share—her need. Once or twice a year, she made the rounds of musical performances and strolled the grand avenues and after a week or two was happy to return to the family.

Most of us, however, simply did not know what we were missing. Work was at the center of daily life, and, by and large, relaxation was equated with idleness. Farmers never had a complete day of leisure, as animals must be attended, Sunday mornings were reserved for religious services, and the concept of a vacation remained just that, a concept, for most Winzigers. We were delighted when master-baker Schilk reserved a corner of his bake shop to serve cakes and coffee or when the school children offered a Christmas play. There was, though, a yearly spectacle loved by Winzigers and appreciated in the entire county, the *Kinderfest*. Although called the children's festival, it was the highlight of the summer and brought thousands of spectators to our town.

There were never more than five or six Jewish families residing in Winzig, too few to employ a rabbi. Nonetheless, they converted a modest building into a synagogue and a cantor or rabbinical student came to lead the congregation on high holy days. An itinerant teacher provided a basic Jewish education to the Jewish children. Until 1934, he had been permitted to use of one of the school rooms for weekly instruction in Hebrew, Jewish history, and, for the boys, Bar Mitzvah preparation. I was not his favorite student. At age eight or nine, I had asked the poor man why God needed us to keep telling Him how great He was—didn't He know that already?

Winzig provided the necessities of life, its rhythm was predictable, its services considered adequate by most of the people. Could we not boast a stop on the railroad line, as well as daily bus service to Breslau? Did we not have a hospital run by soft-spoken Catholic nuns and a post office guarded by the fierce, Prussian black eagle over the door? Did not the Lutherans and Catholics take pride in their churches, securely anchored amid the neat graves of their cemeteries? A Jewish cemetery attested to a long history of a Jewish presence in town; my grandfather's grave remains there among the once-tidy plots.

CHAPTER 2

ZU HAUSE (AT HOME)

My family, the Steinhardts, shared a house with our Moses relations.
My father's sister, my Aunt Anna, had married my mother's brother,
my Uncle Jakob. Thus, the Moses and Steinhardt children shared the
same grandparents. The two brothers-in-law were partners in several,
varied business enterprises. My father ran the farming and cattle trading
ventures. Uncle Jakob managed investments and traveled to Breslau
every Monday to conduct business at the stock exchange. The youngest
of the Moses children, Margot, was only a few months older than I. We
grew up like sisters. Sometimes, our mothers dressed us in identical
outfits and we might be mistaken to be twins. Margot and I shared our
happy, pre-Nazi childhood, and remained together until the summer of
1938. The companionship and love we shared was a priceless gift and
perhaps responsible for our survival of the Hitler years without profound
emotional scarring.

Our roots in Winzig were as identical as our twinned outfits. Both
families had come to Winzig when the German province of Posen was
awarded to Poland by the 1919 Treaty of Versailles ending the First
World War. Their families had lived in that area for as long as anyone
could remember, but German was their language, their customs, and

their loyalty. So, they sold their properties and moved across the new border to Winzig. My father purchased a complex of buildings that had once been used as a Prussian armory. The structures were remodeled and became the living quarters of some twenty-five rooms for both families, Steinhardts on the first floor, Moses on the second, though we were constantly in and out of each other's rooms. We had ample space, gas and electricity connections, even a telephone. Yet, the house could make no claim for comfort. Water had to be pumped into the kitchens from a well, most of the house was without heat, and a dozen people shared a single toilet. The lone bathtub was busy on Friday afternoons when same-sex cousins were scrubbed in the same water. During the winters, the water froze in the bedroom wash-basins. Many cold evenings we held our feather comforters against the warm tiles of the stove, and, clutching them, ran to our beds. Nonetheless, compared to most of our neighbors, we were well-off. A wall of shelves stored my mother's colorful jars of preserved fruits and vegetables, a cabinet made of wire netting allowed apples to dry without rotting, a bag of sour milk in a hallway dripped as it turned into wonderful cheese. We took turns at the butter churn. The walls were deep enough to create window seats where the readers in the family curled up. A rather pretentious silver samovar decorated the large dining room table, and the back hall was wide enough to hold a half dozen bicycles. For several years, we had a car and driver, used mainly for excursions. Horse and buggy were my father's preferred transportation on his trips to nearby villages.

The property was extensive. Connected to the living quarters were a bakery, a steam- powered flour mill, and a machine shop. These buildings stood at right angles to the hayloft, the barns, and the chicken coop. In a corner, half hidden by lilac bushes, were three outhouses to be used by the men in the family and the hired help. Beyond the yard, my Papa had created one of the finest gardens in the vicinity. His flowers, fruits, and vegetables and the generosity with which he shared his bounty earned applause from even the most taciturn of neighbors. His red roses shared the same petite trees with white and pink blossoms. Different kinds of apples ripened on their own branches of the same tree. His dahlias were the size of dinner plates, and his half acre of strawberries were everyone's favorite desert. His took particular pride in the rows upon rows of asparagus, rarely cultivated in our area. Each year, in the early morning of the first Sunday in May, many neighborhood children waited for my Papa at his garden gate. They followed him along the yellow clay paths bordered by thousands of narcissi. Each child was given a bouquet for his or her mother on her special day.

My father had a taste for the exotic. A peacock named Audi, and his peahen, Frau Audi, roamed the grounds. Someone had brought an abandoned baby deer that grew to maturity in his private paddock. A pair of midget-sized prairie chickens with feathered feet reared tiny chicks from their pigeon-sized eggs. Papa studied beekeeping and set up four hives that produced the sweetest honey. Horses, cows, pigs, goats, a pony, a variety of fowl, dogs, and cats completed our animal world. The children in the family were as comfortable with them as they were with each other. I was around ten years old when I happened to go into the barn and heard a peculiar cry from the pen of our pregnant goat. I found her in the throes of birthing. She had delivered a kid, but not been able to rip open its amniotic sac. I managed to do it, but the kid was dead. Then came another one, and, rather uncommonly, one more. Mother goat and I made sure they got air, then I brought the ninny some wet mash. Papa was proud of me and declared the kids were mine. I was very happy with my gift, so I put ribbons around their necks, which they promptly chewed off each other. A few months later, they ate my brother Friedel's raincoat. leaving nothing but the buttons. He was so angry, he refused to speak to me for a week.

Before the rise of the Nazis, I was not aware of anti-Semitism. It existed; my parents used a word that sounded like "*rishis*" when referring to certain people and I had figured out it meant "hater of Jews," but the word was spoken as an observation as one may note the day's weather. There was some socializing between Jews and gentiles, usually to celebrate some special family event. On such occasions, my father bowed from the waist and kissed the ladies' hands, much to the displeasure of my mother. But couples did not make appointments to go out with other couples; indeed, aside from the taverns, there was no place to go. Most evenings, our neighbor Hugo Kliem came to sit a while in our kitchen. He owned a substantial farm and his family had lived in Winzig for five centuries. A handsome man with bright blue eyes, he had a ruddy complexion and a neat, white beard. He usually arrived after the evening milking. He sat by the window and talked about promising heifers, obstinate sows, the evils of the political scene, and, of course, the state of the crops in the fields. My Papa, who got up before five every morning, would wish him a good night around 8 pm and Herr Kliem would leave. Many years later, it occurred to me that Herr Kliem had a crush on my mother and was content just to be near her, just to look at her.

When I reached the maturity to understand that my parents were individuals, I realized they loved one another despite their contrasting personalities. Theirs was not a marriage made in heaven, not a romantic match, but a union grounded in pragmatism. In today's jargon, they would be judged incompatible. My mother loved music and she had a beautiful voice. The priest of the village where she grew up had allowed her, a Jewish girl, to perform the solos in his church choir. The great Italian operatic tenor Enrico Caruso was her hero; she cherished Sunday afternoons when the radio featured performances from the famed opera houses in Berlin and Vienna. My father was indifferent to this important part of her world; her one attempt to have him share her passion was a total failure when he snored during a performance of *Carmen*. But, every so often, my Papa did sing, usually after a day away on business, always the same Polish ditty no one would translate for me. Then my Mutti would smile and say something like:

"Aha, good, your day went well."

My Mother read romantic novels, my Papa read the newspaper and seed catalogues. She paid attention to style, he took no notice of fashion.

Some winter evenings, we children would sit quietly as she, accompanied by Hansi, her canary, sang operatic arias for us. Mutti was a little plump with black, curly hair set off by smooth, white skin. But under that feminine exterior was a core of toughness, a no-nonsense approach to what needed to done. She proved this many times, including shortly after my entry into the world.

When I was born, as was customary, a nurse was brought into the house to take care of me. The lovely *Schwester* (sister—a title given to German nurses) Baer was young, slim, always in starched whites. She slept in my nursery and the length of her stay was expected to be two years. But my father's eye, and I suspect more than his eye, had been attracted to her. Mutti waited until Papa left on one of his cattle buying trips to Pomerania to tell the *Schwester* to pack up and leave—now! When my father returned he was faced with an accomplished fact. "I decided that one year here is long enough for *Schwester*." No consultation, no tears, no confrontation, no fuss at all.

My father's personality might have given a psychologist a headache as well. He was inordinately admiring of power, of titles, and of wealth, while at the same time quite capable of defying authority. Mutti had no patience with his pride of having befriended some baron or almost-millionaire. Her retort was a pithy, "*Er macht auch krumme Beine wenn er kackt*," which rather roughly translates to, "He too must bend his legs when he sits on the toilet." But her words were spoken without rancor because she knew that not even the Kaiser himself could threaten her husband's devotion to his family.

My mother was atypical of most country women. She never milked a cow in her life. The great majority of Winzig farmers' wives left their beds before sun-up, lit a fire in the stove, hauled water from the pump in the street, sliced the bread they baked yesterday, made the coffee (not from expensive coffee beans but from roasted barley), helped with the milking, and saw to the children, all before eight o'clock. At noon, the men came for the main meal of the day, potatoes and vegetables, supplemented once or twice a week with meat. Afternoons found these women, their hands callused, their backs bent, weeding the garden, feeding the pigs and chickens. At dusk, they returned to the milking stool, and, finally, prepared a cold supper. And then there was washday. In my family, we changed our clothes once a week, but that was deemed excessive by most Winzigers. Laundry was usually a monthly chore, one that exhausted even the young and the strong; as so many pails of water had to be pumped, carried into the house, and heated. The scrubbing board and coarse soap rubbed skin off knuckles. During winters, laundry hung on clotheslines froze into sharp-edged rigidity by evening. The next day, baskets of linens were taken to the *Mangel,* a hand-operated monster of an appliance with heavy rollers that smoothed out wrinkles.

Merchants' wives worked hard too. They were active in business long before the so-called liberation of their gender. Beside home-making and child rearing, they scrubbed the sidewalk in front of the store, helped serve customers, kept accounts, and washed the windows and floors. It was common practice that upon the death of the husband, widows continued to run various establishments on their own.

My mother worked in a unique way. She and my father were partners in several business ventures, which included cattle and horse trading, the sale of grain and fertilizer, a steam-driven flour mill, and a bakery. In addition, there were fields to be planted and harvested, the garden to be tended, and the animals in the barns to give time and energy. Help was easily available, as there was no shortage of workmen seeking employment during the Weimar Republic. But, while both my parents were financially savvy, my father preferred staying close to the soil and the animals, while my mother, literally, kept her hands warm with commerce. Mornings would find her in her starched, white apron counting breads and rolls as they left the bakery oven; she then supervised the transfer of the baked goods to awaiting horse-drawn wagons lined up in the yard. Notebook in hand, she told each of the drivers how much he was expected to sell that day and which villages were on his route.

Sales were brisk because "store bread" saved the village women the chore of baking their own. Whispers hinted that at night the wagons served young lovers as well. Decades later, I asked my oldest brother if it was true. Walter smiled and said:

"There were always lots of empty sacks on the floor."

"You mean the ones used to pack up next day's the bread and rolls? You didn't!"

"More comfortable than the bushes. Especially in the rain."

Although I had never met a professional woman during my childhood, some of the girls I knew hoped for careers—usually with unspoken maternal support. I remember the day my cousin Ruth, Margot's older sister, passed her *Abitur*, the exam required for university admission. Ruth sent her parents a telegram and when my Aunt Anna read it aloud, my mother cried. They were tears of joy and pride. My Mutti never spoke of her own impossible dream, to be a professional singer. Women of her generation rarely sought careers of their choosing, but perhaps Ruth might breathe the rarefied air of liberation.

Ruth was the eldest of the Steinhardt-Moses children, two years older than my brother Walter. Her education had was typical for the Weimar years when academic knowledge was respected. Of course, the old stand-bys: emphasis on good behavior, neat handwriting, and erect posture in our seats, had not been seriously challenged. Some teachers in Winzig's public school, like Rektor Johannes Spieler, the principal, encouraged us to think about the material we were learning, but drills and memorization continued to be our usual fare. Our parents accepted our grades with little comment or reproach; a nod, if we did well, a halfhearted, "Is that your best?" if the grades reflected our boredom. Reports of unruly behavior in the classroom, however, were not tolerated and likely to result in punishment. My second brother, built square and solid, called Dicker—meaning Fatso—was not promoted from kindergarten to first grade. My parents' reaction: "The teacher knows best."

After the last school bell of the day released us, we went home to our eat dinner and then did as we pleased. The boys competed in endless games of soccer, flew kites, and ran foot races. The girls played hopscotch or tag, dressed baby farm animals in doll's clothing, read, or did nothing at all. Hide and seek was a favorite for both boys and girls. Among our hiding places were treetops and horse stalls. No one supervised us. We were expected to manage our time without adult interference and neither my mother nor my father considered it their duty to entertain or supervise us. I do not recall my mother or father even checking our homework. If one of us had been foolish enough to say "I'm bored," the response would have been, "I have a chore for you." We had a few toys, but the Moses and Steinhardt children in particular were avid readers, particularly during the long winters.

Our parents were not inclined to engage in soul-searching conversations with us, nor did they try to mold us according to some current standard of child perfection. In retrospect, I realize they accepted the role of heredity to be dominant in child development. Conversation around the dinner table frequently involved our resemblance to certain relatives and the ways in which our strength and failings compared to this uncle or that cousin. It was generally accepted in Winzig that nature, not nurture formed the basis of personality. How fortunate to have ambitious, cheerful, kind, and loving offspring; how unlucky if the son was cruel or the daughter morose. Disappointing, of course, but the fault was not placed at the parental door. "That's just how the child is." This view may explain the serious interest in the *Kinderstube* of marriage prospects. Literally translated the word means "the children's room," but it connotes a person's family background, including mental and physical health, morality, and temperament. It was perfectly acceptable for parents to investigate the *Kinderstube* of a potential son- or daughter-in-law. If undesirable traits were discovered on the family tree, the relationship might be broken off without rancor on either side.

Rarely were we children asked how we spent the day. Our quarrels and tribulations were ours to resolve. We were expected to appear punctually at meals with washed hands and faces and combed hair. If we got too noisy at the table, Papa quieted us with a mere glance toward the top of the china closet where a horse whip was kept. On rare occasions, usually because of complaints from neighbors or teachers, it was deemed necessary to apply that whip to one of the boys' bottom. But my brothers came prepared. When they obediently leaned across the seat of a chair, it would be with a pillow stuffed inside their pants. Papa knew, but did not let on that he knew, and went through the sham of a caning. Not counting an occasional smack on the rear, I was never struck by my parents. But as the youngest and the only girl, I lodged many complaints against my siblings. My mother ignored my grievances or told me, "Go and sit on the green couch and pout." At bedtime, she inspected our toothbrushes to see if they had been used, and then said good night. Of course, we had wet them without applying them to our teeth. I knew I was loved, yet I sometimes wished for a different, gentler, less aloof mother; one who demonstrated greater affection. No wonder I enjoyed being sick, for then I was given Mutti's undivided attention.

How fortunate that my father was affectionate with us, and especially so with me. He probably never heard the word "psychology," but he surely had his own method of dealing with my whining. Sitting on his knee, I would plead my case, perhaps underlined by a few tears: Dicker broke my doll, Friedel said I couldn't play soccer with the boys, and more of the same. Papa would seem incensed that such an injustice had been done to me. He would bang the table with his fist. Then he would shout:

"Such misbehavior must be punished. For an entire week, he"—whoever was the day's offender—"will have to go to bed without shoes and socks on!"

I would prance away, satisfied by the tone of his voice. It was years before I actually realized what he had said. By then, I was old enough to appreciate Papa's diplomacy.

But Papa showed confidence in all his children. Once, he told Dicker, then age 14, to fetch a cow my father had purchased in a nearby village, about five miles from Winzig. My brother grumbled but set out. On foot. On a hot summer day. No one said a word about being careful, or taking some water, or resting under a tree if he got tired. Dicker simply went and paid for the cow. He got hold of the rope around her neck and started out for home. But this Bessie did not want to walk. Dicker pulled and pushed and twisted her tail. She took two steps, and then stood glued to the ground. Some of the villagers gathered and snickered. This was quite entertaining! How humiliating for young Steinhardt! Then, one of the spectators asked, "How much do you want for this worthless beast?" My brother added a reasonable profit to the cost and named his price. They shook hands; the deal was made. With the money in his pocket, my brother walked the five miles home, admittedly a little nervous. But Papa laughed and said, "Well done."

But the child rearing methods applied by the Steinhardt and Moses families were not the norm in Winzig. I often saw classmates with welts or bruises. Asked what happened, the most likely response was a shrug of the shoulder and "I forgot to do...and my father got mad." Spanking was acceptable, hitting with belts or ropes deemed harsh, but understandable. The right of a parent to be obeyed without question was anchored in the rationale that respect for authority was the glue that held society together. This was Prussia, the German state that had unified the nation by fighting and winning three wars. The chancellor who had lead that struggle, Otto von Bismark (1815–1898), was known as the Iron Chancellor and the "iron" refers to the guns used to achieve his political goal. In the minds of most Prussians, the army became the vaunted instrument to achieve greatness. Victory in battle depended on the compliance of soldiers to the command of their officers. Thus, in civil life, children must obey parents. The concept of following orders without reservation took on an aura of sacred obligation for many Prussians.

So, it was generally accepted that some children, usually the disobedient ones, had to "learn the hard way." Every teacher in the lower grades had a cane. On occasion—mostly for talking out of turn—I, too, stood before the class with my upturned hand to receive my three strokes. Boys were punished more severely; they stood doubled over. As long as Rektor Spieler was the principal, further brutality against students was not tolerated, but when the faculty was Nazified, harsh new rules were implemented. At that point, the Prussian ideal of unquestioned compliance became absolute.

Children submitted to parents and teachers. Adults submitted to work. The farmland in this region of Silesia demanded the virtual enslavement of its workers to produce a modest income. Still, unending toil was no guarantee of economic survival: weather; market prices for milk, grains, and potatoes; interest rates on everlasting loans; health of livestock; cost of fertilizers; and a variety of unforeseen disasters decided whether a farmer could hang on for another year. Even so, nothing was more central to him than land ownership. Never mind that the fields produced a new crop of rocks after each plowing. Never mind that the soil was too wet, too welcoming to weeds, too sandy, or too hilly—it bound its owner with the power of a magnet, generation after generation. Self-respect and social status were invested in ownership and the dread of foreclosure was an ever-present threat for many Winzigers. The majority of children left school at sixteen, as Winzig, like many small towns, offered no further public education. Most hoped for work as apprentices to craftsmen, but found jobs as maids or store clerks or farm labor. The sons and some of the daughters of the professional and business community were not tied by the same tether, their future offered greater opportunities. My cousins, brothers, and I were reared to expect careers, not merely jobs. But when Walter said he wanted to become a dentist, my father was appalled. The idea of his son spending his life with his hands in other peoples' mouths seemed to Papa most undignified. There were many heated arguments.

I hated to hear them shout in anger and looked for a quiet spot to lose myself in a book, any book. A favorite one was an encyclopedia hidden in the back of the book case. Sex education did not exist, so I learned what I could by trying to decipher the diagrams and long words. My parents did not discuss procreation at all. Poultry mating didn't help because it was impossible to relate what happened between the rooster and the hen to the human bedroom. I must have been nine or ten when I knew something unusual was about to happen because my father ordered all the wagons and equipment that usually cluttered the yard be cleared away. That done, he led one of our horses, a fine-looking stallion, into the enclosure. One of our workers noticed me sitting on the branch of our great oak tree. He turned to my father:

"Herr Steinhardt, look, there is Rita."

After a moment, Papa said: "She can stay. She's old enough."

A moment later, our neighbor Herr Kliem came through the gate leading one of his mares on a short halter. The stallion picked up his ears and his gait turned into a dance. The mare's ears and eyes rolled, giving her a fierce and wild look. Both animals whinnied, and the whites of their eyes seemed huge as they threatened to break loose from their bridles. Something was turning them into fierce, unfamiliar creatures. Even in the safety of the tree, I was frightened. The stallion approached the mare. I saw Papa and Herr Kliem nod with approval. Then, I noticed, protruding from the stallion's underbelly, the male sex organ was much enlarged, almost touching the ground. It had become engorged to the thickness of our largest garden hose. With my hands over my face, I watched the mating through spread fingers. Afterward, the horses calmed down and were led away, but I did not move from my perch for some time.

I did not speak about this experience to anyone, but several weeks later Walter asked me to sit in the garden with him. He had won his arguments and was soon going off to Berlin to study dentistry, but wanted to have a talk before he left. Actually, he wanted to have THE talk. He spoke of sex as an expression of love between men and women, he answered my questions, and he reassured me that violence was not the norm when people made love. He did not need to stress the importance of virginity, I already knew pregnancy of an unmarried girl spelled disaster for her and her family; she forfeited her chances of a good marriage; she and her child would forever bear the stigma of her sin. Even in Winzig, there were cases of young women who chose suicide over a life of shame. I accepted the taboo of premarital sex completely and was middle-aged before I asked myself: How and why were sex and sin yoked together?

CHAPTER 3

HOW DID I BECOME
AN *UNTERMENSCH?*

During the early morning of the first day in April of 1933, I noticed several pairs of SA men standing at the doors and gates leading to our property. They seemed to loiter, stomping their feet, smoking, chatting; only their uniforms were impressive. Were they guarding our house? Then, I saw the clubs their hands. I felt a twinge in my stomach, not quite a pain, but more than mere discomfort. That twinge was the beginning of a distress that would plague me for many years. I ran to tell my mother about the brownshirts.

We stood together by the window and noted these troopers were local boys, but wearing heavy boots and belts they seemed different. It would take several months before we understood their new outfits changed more than their appearance; their attitudes displayed a new self-assurance, their stride showed a new confidence, their behavior indicated a new callousness.

Mutti shrugged her shoulders.

"So this is the boycott? Here in Winzig? I can't believe they'd bother with us," she shook her head, more surprised than upset.

"What is a boycott?" I asked.

She explained the recently installed chancellor, a certain Herr Hitler, was trying to prevent Christians from doing business with Jews. The man was an anti-Semite, one who hates the Jews. This boycott was supposed to keep our customers away. I shook my head. Why should someone in Berlin care who used our mill or shopped in our bakery? Mutti touched my hair and assured me our regulars would ignore this display; they were loyal; there was nothing to worry about.

Mutti was mistaken. Within a few minutes, we witnessed the first of many lessons that it was unwise to underestimate Adolf Hitler, that Austrian corporal. A horse-drawn wagon with sacks of grain drew up in front of the gate near the mill. The driver expected to grind some of last year's wheat into flour, a service he had used before. One of the SA men stepped forward and snatched the halter of the man's horse. We could not hear the exchange of words, but clearly the driver was ordered to leave. Puzzled and annoyed, the farmer shouted and lifted his whip, perhaps to urge his horse forward, perhaps to threaten the trooper. That brought a second brownshirt into the argument. Fists were raised. We heard some more unintelligible cursing and then the wagon backed away. Now we both understood what a boycott was. Mutti's face had paled and my stomach hurt.

That evening, the situation took a more serious turn. Our friend and neighbor, Hugo Kliem, came for his usual evening visit and was stopped at the entrance gate. Herr Kliem became furious and berated the troopers with his most colorful Silesian invective. Not only did he call their parentage into question, the word *Schweinehund* (swinedog) was clearly audible, shouted back and forth. When Herr Kliem pushed the men aside, they struck him several times. He kept going and came into our kitchen, bleeding from the head. My mother, with trembling fingers, tended to his cuts. She begged him not to come again. He shook his head:

"I will cut a hole in the fence where our gardens meet. After dark. If you need shopping, give me a list and I'll take care of it."

Officially, the boycott was scheduled to last one day, and that was generally the case. But not in Winzig. The newly appointed mayor, Joachim Lang, was also the local Nazi Party chief. He kept his SA men at our doors for two months. By the time they were withdrawn, the bakery and mill were no longer viable businesses. Herr Kliem reported that the mayor was ambitious to make Winzig the first town in county to be declared *Judenrein* (cleansed of Jews). He sent Winzig's single policeman, Herr Urban, to close down the bakery. When he placed the seal on the lock, the bins of flour and cans of yeast were still filled, food for cockroaches for years to come. The sign he posted on the door read: **Closed for sanitary violations**. There had been no inspection of the premises.

Mayor Lang, who had done menial labor for my father in his youth, also delighted in ordering Papa's frequent arrest. Herr Urban was embarrassed to lock him in the cell in the basement of city hall so often. My mother chose me to bring the "prisoner" his meals, as she worried my brothers could be arrested as well. Proudly, yet nervously, I brought Papa baskets of food. I sat on his narrow cot while my father ate and entertained me with stories of his two cell mates—flies he had named Max and Moritz. Never maudlin, he was certain no charges could be brought against him. Indeed, he was always released in a day or two.

Several members of our small synagogue congregation began to make arrangements to leave Germany. During the early 1930s, it was difficult but not yet impossible to find a refuge. Emigrants could still take some assets with them, but the majority of German Jews lacked such foresight. My father's attitude was rather typical on that issue:

"The German people will soon get rid of this Austrian nobody. Our country has a solid Constitution, our people are educated. How long will they tolerate this charlatan to head the government? Just wait until the next election, Hitler will be gone."

That there might not be another fair election was unthinkable in 1933. My father's flawed logic was but one among a number of rationalizations why one could not leave the fatherland: How can one simply abandon aging relatives; lose a pension; sell assets at a loss? The children were too young; it was too late in life to learn another language; there is no time to study for professional qualifications in another country...and so forth and so forth. Only half of the Jews of Germany left in time to escape the Holocaust. During the first several years of Hitler's dictatorship, the idea that the Fuehrer might solve the so-called "Jewish question" by mass murder was simply beyond belief. It was not until November 9 of 1938, when a pogrom known as Crystal Night made it clear that flight was no longer a choice, but a necessity. By then, the exodus would have involved some eight hundred thousand German and Austrian Jews. The number accepted by the nations of the world was dwarfed by the number refused even temporary refuge.

My mother was willing to share Papa's "sit tight and wait" non-action, but she worried about Walter and Dicker. The Nuremberg Laws of 1935 had deprived Jews of their citizenship and that included to right to an education. Then, a rumor was circulated that the Nazis planned to perform some dreadful medical experiments on young Jewish men. Even if her husband was right, Mutti knew her older sons needed a safe haven until the danger passed. The notion that Friedel and I might be in danger seemed absurd, this, after all, was not Tsarist Russia—the Germans were a civilized people and surely would not harm children.

Month by month, sometimes week by week, a flood of new decrees transformed our lives. Children were on the front lines of the impact of many anti-Jewish decisions made by the Fuehrer and his circle. The Nazis regarded the classroom as the essential arena for the creation of their Thousand Year Third Reich. The young must be trained to assure this millennium. First on that agenda: a total overhaul of the educational system. A new decree ordered the dismissal of all Jewish or otherwise "unreliable" teachers. From grade schools to universities, the profession was made *Judenrein* as quickly as replacements could be found. Public education was (and is) a federal responsibility in Germany and thus a single law ended the careers of thousands of educators throughout the nation. Staffs were "purified" by the dismissal of anyone declared untrustworthy, such as educators with past memberships in anti-Nazi political organizations. Instructors who were permitted to continue their work were ordered to attend many hours of training on the recently mandated Nazi methods of education.

New textbooks were printed and the traditional German school system vanished. The most intensive attention was given to the "science" of racial studies. Aryan superiority was at the core of all lessons. Jews who had authored German literature or were renowned scientists, musicians, or philosophers had their names and accomplishments expunged. Heinrich Heine presented a problem. His poem, *Die Lorelei,* was a national treasure and too well-loved to simply disappear. Our new textbook contained the poem but the credit line read: Author Unknown. The concept that Aryan culture, meaning German culture, was the mainspring of every advance made by mankind was the basic theme of every course. It is no exaggeration to state education became a tool of propaganda minister Josef Goebbels.

Obedience, and specifically total obedience to the Fuehrer, was an essential part of Nazi education. Linked to that concept was emphasis on physical strength and the glorification of war. Woe to the student who could not climb the rope or jump the hurdle. When might makes right, power justifies itself through victory over the weak. Models from nature were regular illustrations—animals from the lion to the fox hunt and kill their prey without guilt or pity, ergo...

For Jewish children, classrooms became arenas of humiliation and confusion. Cousin Margot and I had accepted the authority of our teachers as absolute and sat quietly as all but one of our teachers, Rektor Spieler, lectured enthusiastically on the criminality of the Jewish race. We learned Jews are the natural enemies of Aryans, that they are dangerous, manipulative, amoral, and most unwelcome in the Reich. Herr Mai, who always wore his swastika pin on his lapel, was particularly malicious. He looked pleased when he instructed the class on the correct execution of the "Heil Hitler" salute and announced that, of course, Jews are excluded from this revered rite. Some months later, he announced that henceforth my cousin and I, eleven years old, need not bother to raise our hands in class, he would not call on us again. Shortly thereafter, he moved our seats to the back of the room. Some of our classmates looked at us with sympathy as we made our way to the rear, others smiled with satisfaction. One dared to ask:

"Herr *Lehrer,* (teacher), why?"

Mai replied: "Jews, by their nature, pollute those near them."

Nearly every day, he launched into examples of Jewish criminality. On one occasion he asked: "You know about the recent shortage of onions in the nation, don't you? The price is sky high. You wonder, what is the reason for that? I will tell you. The Jews. They bought up the whole crop so now we have to pay twice as much as before."

On that very day, I walked into our kitchen to find my own mother in the act of committing treason. She was chopping an onion. I burst into tears and for a moment my mother was speechless, as I so rarely cried.

Mutti put aside her work, sat down, and asked what was wrong. Neither Margot nor I had told our parents how former friends now shunned us. We hadn't revealed how our teachers repeated again and again that Jews were the cause of every problem facing the country: the loss of the Great War, unemployment, inflation, depression, the Bolshevik menace —whatever ailed the fatherland, the Jews were responsible. The fact that German Jewry accounted for less than one percent of the German population of sixty million was never mentioned; the impression was fostered that the Jewish presence was much larger. Margot and I consoled one another simply by being together. I cannot recall any conversation with an adult about the contempt we faced every day. We were not ready to think that teachers could be liars, so Margot and I decided that our families were different, they were good, unlike those other Jews, the wicked ones, whoever, wherever they might be. *Die Juden sind unser Unglueck*, the Jews are our misfortune, was repeated so often, not just in school but in the newspapers, on the radio, on posters, everywhere we looked—it was inconceivable that it could be a lie.

I might have used this moment with my mother to share my confusion and humiliation, but I did not. I simply could not. No words would form, but Mutti was waiting and finally I told her Herr Mai said Jews are responsible for the onion shortage. Mutti's answer came quickly:

"You know we grow our own vegetables, never buy them. These onions came from our garden. Your father raises animals and grain, many products are needed in the country. Herr Mai is mistaken."

I felt a little better. Mutti stroked my hair and asked if some of the children or teachers were hateful toward Margot or me; if they said or did spiteful things. Her voice was unusually high and she fastened her eyes on mine. I looked away, then shrugged my shoulders and went to my room.

How could I explain what I did not understand myself? Had my brother Walter been home, he might have helped me, but Walter was studying dentistry in Berlin. So, I did what I usually did when troubled, I climbed onto my favorite window seat and reached for my solace—a book. Or else, I would lose myself in my favorite daydream: I became a German heroine, beautiful and athletic, winner of many medals in the upcoming Olympic Games. I would bring honor and pride to the nation and Herr Mai, even Herr Hitler, would admit they had been wrong about the Jewish people. And then Irene would be my friend again.

Irene, cousin Margot, and I had been inseparable. We had walked to school together, and, after the last bell of the day, looked for one another to play. Starting in 1934, though, Irene changed. Gradually, over several months, our friend became our tormentor. The shift occurred in steps. First, she no longer played with us. Then, she joined the Nazi youth group for girls, the BDM, *Bund Deutscher Maedel*, and wore her BDM uniform to school. She walked away when Margot or I tried to speak to her. Finally, Irene joined some other girls who called us names and spat on the ground as they passed us on the street. I thought about Irene constantly, with anger, with hatred, with visions of revenge, and with dreams of reconciliation. It would take a decade or more for these images of Irene to fade.

Rektor Spieler, meanwhile, had an "Irene" of his own. As principal of the school, Herr Rektor was an impressive figure, tall, with the erect bearing of a former soldier, steel-gray hair, and a matching mustache. He was popular with parents and students, an excellent instructor and administrator who served Winzig for twenty-five years. But, his politics were wrong. He was a Democrat, not a Nazi. Beginning in 1933, his life was made unbearable by Georg Mai, the most ardent supporter of the Fuehrer on Winzig's faculty, a man ambitious to see his name on the door of the principal's office. He instigated and pursued a campaign against Rektor Spieler that dragged on for several years. Among the charges against the Rektor were such criminal acts as permitting the itinerant Hebrew teacher the use a classroom to instruct the Jewish children; tardiness in replacing the black-red-gold flag of the Republic with the newly issued swastika; insistence on punishment of an Aryan boy who beat a Jewish child (my brother Friedel) on school grounds; and similar offenses. Nothing in the complaints questioned Spieler's professional performance. Though not listed in the denunciations, but certainly remembered by the Nazis, was the Rektor's role in the fiasco of the 1934 *Kinderfest.*

Winzig's existence was based on agriculture but the endless require-ments of fields and animals were interrupted for just one weekend every summer. For two days the town shed its work clothes and trans-formed itself into a place of color, music, and enjoyment—the *Kinderfest* (Children's Festival). The celebration would begin with a parade from the school to the *Lustgarten*, the forest, three miles from town. Many hundreds of visitors and Winzigers lined the streets to applaud the marching bands, the riders on garlanded horses, the wheels of bicycles flashing with colored ribbons, the farm wagons transformed into brilliant floats by blankets of flowers. Not only did the schoolchildren march in the parade, but also the members of the medieval craft guilds. Butchers, shoemakers, gravediggers, and blacksmiths, each contingent was dressed according to its trade, from chimneysweeps all in black, to bakers all in white. All eyes were on the festival queen as she passed beneath her crown of cornflowers held high by her four maids of honor. The queen had won this tribute by earning the highest score in the competition of girls' sports and games. Every girl in Winzig envied her. Crowds of spectators followed the procession to a clearing in the forest where tables and chairs had been set up under the trees. The music never stopped, food and drink were served or emptied from baskets, and children's laughter added to the delight of the day.

Rektor Spieler had been appointed marshal of the *Kinderfest* in 1934. His preparations had begun months before the June date. The weather was perfect, the procession beautiful. Margot and I marched with our class, side by side in our new outfits. Throughout the day, we ran and jumped, shot our arrows, and participated in games. At dusk, the girl who had won the greatest number of competitions was to be named the festival queen. But, that announcement was not made at the usual time. What was the delay? Clearly, there was a problem. The problem was cousin Margot. She had earned the royal honor, she was the best female athlete in the school! What happened to Aryan superiority? Herr Mai fumed; it was simply not possible to have a Jewish queen. Margot was asked if was willing to rescind her right to be crowned. She said, "No." Just one word: "No."

During the heated discussion that followed, Rektor Spieler pulled out the regulations manual and asked Herr Mai to show him a rule that would deny the award on religious grounds. But, the rules had not been updated to exclude non-Aryans. The Rektor stood his ground. Margot was pronounced the queen. Now, she needed four maids of honor to escort her on the lantern-lit march home. Of course, I would be one, but who else would serve? Though usually considered a privilege, none of our own classmates agreed to serve as a maid of honor. Eventually, we settled for the services of three younger girls we barely knew. Thus, Margot had her moment of victory, bittersweet though it was.

This was the last *Kinderfest* for Margot and me. The following year, we watched through a window curtain as the corn-flowered crown was carried to the forest without a queen. Our defender, Rektor Spieler, suffered an increase of attackers when Mayor Lang aligned his clique to join Herr Mai's effort to oust the Rektor. They brought charges against him that went from court to court as proceedings dragged on in endless requests for depositions, interrogations, legal maneuvering, and the prejudice of regional officials. It exhausted Spieler. Nonetheless, he continued to defend himself; it was a matter of principle for him. He took his case all the way to the national education minister, Dr. Bernhard Rust. A ministerial investigation found Spieler innocent of malfeasance. But, the struggle had made life in Winzig impossible for the performance of his duties and had hurt his family. The Rektor accepted the offer of a transfer to a school in another town, to Maltsch. On the day he vacated his office, Herr Mai moved in.

Without the Rektor, Margot and I, the only Jewish children in the school, were without protection from teachers or classmates. Herr Mai felt free to give his lesson on *Rassenkunde,* racial studies, a personal touch. He called to the front of the room a blonde, blue-eyed classmate, and Mai used a tape measure and determined the size of her skull; the contour of her face; the length of her nose, forehead, and more. He identified the shade of skin tones, color of eyes, length of earlobes, and so on. He filled half the blackboard with his notations. Then, he called me to the front of the room. (Cousin Margot had brown, curly hair. Mine was black and straight, more typically Semitic.) Mai repeated his theatrical measuring performance on me, and, of course, the results were quite different.

He pointed at the blackboard. "Here, boys and girls," he announced, "you have scientific proof that pure Aryans and Jewish sub-humans are biologically different."

I looked at the floor when returning to my seat, but I held back the tears.

The Nuremberg Laws of 1935 had deprived German Jews of their citizenship. That was merely the beginning. A continuous stream of amendments added an astonishing assortment of prohibitions. Under threat of imprisonment or death, Jews were forbidden to go shopping except during designated hours; blind Jews could not use a service dog or display their white canes; Jews could not keep pets; Jews were barred from parks, museums, theaters, public benches, from owning or using a radio or telephone. Also forbidden was Jewish attendance to concerts, theater, films, or operas. Jews could not travel on public transport, nor could Jews own a weapon, car, or motorcycle. After *Kristallnacht,* Jewish families had to move into designated locations, carry special identity cards, and display the six-pointed stars on their clothing. Most severely punished was the crime of *Rassenschande,* racial defilement, sexual intercourse with an Aryan partner.

Beginning with professional Jews, all opportunities to earn a living were closed off. This list is incomplete, but the point is made. The original goal of the oppression had been to drive the Jews out of the country, then, step by step, the persecution intensified , evolving from "you are not welcome" to "you may not work here" to "you may not live among us," and finally to "you may not live."

When the Steinhardt-Moses businesses were closed by the police, my parents had to be very careful about money. We could no longer afford new clothing, all employees were dismissed, meat was served infrequently. When the coal bin in the basement was empty, Papa chopped wood. Nonetheless, compared to others, we were fortunate. Our garden and my mother's jarred fruits and vegetable kept us well nourished. But how did Papa manage to meet other financial obligations, such as taxes, electric bills, medicines, and the fees required at every step of the emigration process? Years later, he told me his secret.

While it seemed Papa had no income at all, one man remained unafraid to continue to conduct business him. *Rittergutsbesitzer* (a title used to designate ownership of a large estate) Koch took delight in circumventing the Nazis. He also trusted my father absolutely. Koch owned four thousand acres of prime farmland, a fine herd of cattle, several teams of horses, and a riding stable. His milk production had improved markedly under Papa's guidance and suggested changes. Their relationship reached the point where Herr Koch bought animals sight-unseen on Papa's recommendation. When all trade between Jew and Aryan were outlawed, the two men worked out a clandestine arrangement. The not-yet-outlawed telephone would ring in our house. My father would pick up the receiver but say nothing. The caller would not identify himself, just state a time. Our car, horse-drawn carriages, even the motorcycle had been sold or confiscated but we still had some bicycles. Papa would roll one out from the back hallway and off he would go to a meeting place arranged in a previous discussion—an always-different part of the forest where Herr Koch would join him. Thus, the aristocrat and the Jew would come together, one on horseback, the other by bicycle. Their consultations were brief as Papa, who knew every animal on the estate, advised Herr Koch where to buy, and what to sell. For this advice, the *Rittergutsbesitzer* paid Papa a cash commission. The two men were able to maintain this relationship for a year, seeing each other several times a month. But then one of Koch's footmen betrayed his employer to the Nazis. During their last meeting, Koch showed my father a letter he had received from the head of the Nazi party in the village. After the usual "it has been reported that," the letter warned of serious consequences if it were confirmed that the *Rittergutsbesitzer* had had contact with a Jew. The two men shook hands in silence.

Several of our relatives emigrated to Palestine or the United States, but others were not so fortunate. Three who had lost everything came to Winzig to live with us. Aunt Augusta, called Gustchen; was my mother's (and Uncle Jakob's) sister. She was a widow and glad to be with family. Adolph Steinhardt, my Papa's and Aunt Anna's older brother, also arrived. He and his wife moved into in a small apartment carved from larger quarters on the second floor of the house. The couple was childless and kept mostly to themselves. Uncle Adolph, who had been decorated in the Great War, was tall and lean with a somewhat military bearing. I don't recall a single conversation with him.

The Nazi noose was tightening when suddenly, for a few months, the rope slackened. The 1936 Olympics focused the world's attention on Berlin and Germany. Hitler ordered the removal of placards and notices that vilified the Jews. Signs such as "Aryans only" were removed from park benches, overt anti-Semitic speeches and newspaper headlines were muted in the hope that visitors would form a favorable impression of a clean, orderly, revitalized Reich. Some German Jews laid aside their half-hearted plans to leave. Many of them began to think perhaps the worst was over. They were wrong.

CHAPTER 4

FOUR CHILDREN IN FOUR PLACES

The Berlin Olympic Games of 1936 had veiled the most visible Nazi anti-Semitism for a few months, but as soon as the visitors left, Goebbels' propaganda drums increased their invective. New restrictions forced German Jews into further isolation and economic distress. Most of their old Christian friends avoided them; some to prove their loyalty to the Party, others because they feared for their safety and livelihood. Within cities, Jewish day schools increased their enrollments, but, in smaller communities, parents were helpless to protect their children from schoolyard taunts—or worse. As more members of the Hitler Youth wore their uniforms to school, the harassment of their Jewish classmates became a daily ordeal. After *Kristallnacht*, in November of 1938, the government solved this problem by prohibiting all Jewish education, private and public. Each month, the lines around foreign consulates grew longer as the *Untermenschen* sought visas and the wait for these life-saving imprints on a passport page stretched into years.

Many families struggled with contradictory choices. Was it best to send the children out of Germany, perhaps to relatives, perhaps to compassionate strangers, or was it best to keep the family intact? For two years, special trains stopped in Berlin and Vienna to take Jewish children to foster parents in Great Britain. This remarkable volunteer effort, known as the *Kindertransports*, had been initiated through the cooperative efforts of Jewish organizations, the British government, and the Quakers. With the outbreak of Hitler's war, this humanitarian rescue ended, but some 10,000 children had been saved. Ninety percent of these boys and girls were to become orphans. The decision to separate was heart-wrenching. How does a parent explain to a four-year-old why he must be sent away? What about the baby's allergy? Or asthma? Will the children forget us? Can siblings stay together? There were so many questions, and so few reassuring answers. Until the moment of separation, many parents were uncertain they would muster the emotional stamina to actually give their sons and daughters into the arms of strangers.

In retrospect, these were life or death decisions. During the Holocaust, the Nazis murdered one and a half million Jewish children. Even while the *Kindertransports* were carrying their precious freight out of Germany, even then, such a possibility was beyond human imagination. So, mothers and fathers and siblings who were too old to be accepted shouted *"Auf Wiedersehn,"* until we meet again. White handkerchiefs fluttered from the railroad cars and from the hands of those left behind. The British nurses and their aides who accompanied the exodus lifted infants and toddlers for one more look through the windows. When the train was no longer in view, the platform was awash with tears—no need to hold them back any longer. Husbands and wives tried to console each other: "We have done the right thing. Now our *Sonnenschein* (sunshine) will eat nourishing food, have friends to play with, and can walk to school without fear."

My brothers Dicker and Walter were old enough and astute enough to implement their own escapes when it became clear they had no future in Germany. Seventeen-year-old Dicker was accepted into a training site in Holland. HIAS, an international aid organization originally known as the Hebrew Immigrant Aid Society, had funded and established this hands-on facility to prepare young men and women for life and work on a Kibbutz in Palestine. Dicker left without regrets, with just a rucksack on his back. As a son of a farmer, he was reared differently than his comrades from the cities. This gave him an immediate advantage. He loved the work, made new friends and, despite a plentiful diet, he slimmed down. Dicker became Jup, which is Dutch for Josef, his actual name. No longer standing in the shadow of his older brother, Jup discovered pride in his own strengths. His survival during four years of Nazi occupation of the Netherlands confirmed his resourcefulness, courage, and endurance. Fewer than 25 percent of Jews living in Holland survived the brutal policies of Reichskommissar Arthur Seyss-Inquart.

In the spring of 1940, Jup's HIAS group was nearly ready to emigrate to Palestine when the Germans invaded the Netherlands. The Nazi occupation authority immediately revoked the group's permission to emigrate; Jews were no longer permitted to leave. The treatment of the Netherlanders during occupation had been planned to be lenient because Hitler considered the Dutch to be Aryans. However, as it became clear the great majority of the Dutch people hated the invader, German policies grew increasingly harsh. In a country without great forest and no mountains, the Nazi hunt for Jews was dreadfully successful despite the courage of many Dutch citizens who tried to save them. Of the once-thriving, pre-war Jewish population of 140,000, only 30,000 survived. The fate of Anne Frank was replicated thousands of times and one-third of the brave Netherlanders who helped Jews were executed for that crime.

Upon the dissolution of their HIAS group, the young Zionists scattered throughout the country. During nearly five years of German suppression, my brother played many parts. He had mastered the basics of the Dutch language and was fortunate to be accepted into an underground resistance group. The leader of this organization was the owner of a large farm named Sicco L. Mansholt. (He was to become Minister of Agriculture of the Netherlands after the war and later held that post for the European Union.) Jup was issued a variety of false identity papers, and he changed his name, his hair color, and even his gait when on a mission. On his identity papers, Jup was listed as a Dutch farm worker. Unofficially, he carried out anti-Nazi assignments along with his agricultural chores. His unit was engaged in such missions as reporting German military activities to the British, maintaining radio contact with the Dutch Government in exile (in London), derailing German supply trains, and gathering weapons the RAF dropped at night to be used for the group's own defense and for the day the Nazis would be driven from Dutch soil. The Germans suspected Mansholt of his important undercover role and subjected his property to relentless searches. They never discovered the double ceiling of the hay loft, though. A lookout scanned the flat, open landscape constantly and when German soldiers came into view, he used a prearranged signal, a shrill birdcall, which warned the Jewish resistance fighters to disappear into the crawl space. German soldiers drove their bayonets into the mounds of hay in the fields, into the straw stored in barns, into the water troughs of the horses—wherever they thought it was possible for a man or woman to hide. On one occasion, my brother was concealed in a stack of newly cut grain when a bayonet blade passed millimeters from his leg. Another time, one of the soldiers pushed his weapon through the ceiling of the barn where Jews had taken cover. One of the anti-Nazi fighters was struck in the leg. The group had drilled what to do in such an emergency. In an instant, one of the men used his kerchief to wipe the blade clean of blood before it was withdrawn while another comrade used his shirt to prevent the dripping wound from oozing blood through the floorboards. The gash was superficial and it healed without further consequences.

Years later, after Jup and his attractive Dutch bride emigrated to America, we never tired of listening to accounts of his life as a member of the Dutch resistance. During family visits, the children clung to him and begged for one more story. With one or two little ones on his knees, Jup did not resist for long. On one such occasion he asked: "Who can figure out why my comrades and I never left the farm without a straw in our pockets?"

Eventually, after a hint or two, someone came up with the answer:

"You told us Holland has more canals than roads. If you saw a German soldier, you jumped into the water and breathed through the straw!"

"Clever child," beamed Jup.

His most dangerous encounter occurred near the end of the occupation. The English had radioed that a plane was dropping some weapons on this moonless night. Jup was selected to retrieve them. He was riding his bicycle in the direction of the pick-up site when he ran into a German patrol. It was long after curfew and civilians were not permitted on the roads. Two German soldiers ordered Jup off the bike and for several minutes debated what to do with this Dutch *Schweinehund*. They had no idea he understood their conversation and Jup took his clues from their dialogue.

"He looks harmless enough. Too dumb to know what time it is."

"So, what is he doing out this late?"

"Let's see if we can get him to answer. *Was machts Du so spaet?*" ("What are you doing out so late?")

Jup wiped his nose on his sleeve, scratched the seat of his pants, and shouted in Dutch: "Sick cow. Very sick. Need veterinarian."

Eventually, the Germans tired of this uncouth *Dumkopf* (stupid-head) who spat on the ground and used his sleeve to wipe his snotty nose. (Decades later, when the children asked Jup for a demonstration, they laughed ecstatically when he consented.) The soldiers shoved him and his bicycle into their vehicle and drove to their command post. But, no one was at the station to interrogate him. Jup spent the night in a cell. In the morning, for reasons never clear to him, they simply let him go. He even found his bicycle. Upon his return to the farm, he was greeted with much backslapping by his worried comrades.

In 1945, the Canadian armed forces drove the Germans westward and authorized Mr. Mansholt's cadre of underground fighters to participate in the liberation of the Netherlands. When my parents received Jup's first letter, even the agnostics in the family thanked God.

The drama of my brother Walter's flight from Germany played out in a very different setting. He had found a Jewish dentist in Berlin (permitted to treat only Jewish patients) who was willing to take him on while Walter studied dental mechanics. German dentists usually maintained their own laboratories to fabricate crowns, dentures, and such for their patients. Walter divided his time between this practical apprenticeship and university courses at the Dental Institute in Berlin. In an anatomy class, he witnessed an Aryan superiority demonstration. The professor had called a blonde, blue-eyed young man, muscular and obviously athletic, to the podium. He presented him to the class as a model of Aryan superiority. Then, the professor asked the young man his name.

"Jakob Kohn," the student answered. At the sound of this obviously Jewish name, the classroom broke into pandemonium. Naturally, this was a story repeated with glee for months among the anti-Nazis. Sadly, the young man was murdered. He could not be allowed to make a mockery of Aryan superman theories by his very existence.

Walter passed his proficiency exam with honors. Indeed, he was the last Jewish student to be awarded this distinction. But, further education was closed to him by government decree. Fortunately, Walter had become an excellent dental technician and was able to continue to work in that profession. In his spare time, however, he tempted fate.

Though never a card-carrying member of the Communist Party, Walter was much enamored with the ideal of an egalitarian society. The Nazis had outlawed all but their own political party and the first victims to die in German concentration camps were actual and suspected Communists. Walter participated in secret meetings and debates held by a group of followers of Marxism. Among his comrades, only two or three survived. Walter was an effective speaker and lecturer on some aspects of the brave new world these idealists promoted. Their gatherings were routinely publicized as non-political discussions. Walter was speaker at a gathering advertised as a lecture on improving milk production when the door of their meeting room was burst open by several members of the Gestapo (Nazi secret police). Without any change in tone or a missed beat, Walter switched from a condemnation of Nazi policies to the necessity of improving German dairy herds through artificial insemination. He concluded his address to the tumultuous applause of the audience. His boyhood on the farm saved the day, but did not prevent the Gestapo from taking note of Walter's name.

Fortunately, one of my mother's brothers, Uncle Karl, lived in Berlin and kept in touch with a faithful comrade from his service in the First World War. This friend worked at police headquarters and came across the name Walter Steinhardt in a Gestapo file. The friend passed this information to Karl, who urged Walter to leave Germany. Karl even arranged to pay Walter's passage to America. But, like many of his fellows, my brother believed it was important to remain and fight the Nazi menace. Finally, after several narrow escapes, including a trip to Prague to meet with members of a parallel organization, he began to consider emigration. Just for safety's sake, Walter obtained a student visa to an English dental school and secured his passport. He also tried his luck at the American consulate. Early one morning, he joined the line of people seeking refuge in the United States. There, he met his first great love, Rahli. As Walter told the story:

> I had come early and secured a place near the entrance to the building. After standing there for about two hours, I noticed a strikingly attractive girl passing the queue towards the far end. Never reluctant to pursue and approach a pretty wench, I turned to the person next to me, "There is my sister, looking for me. I'll be back with her in a moment."

> I ran to catch up with this modem Venus, seized her arm, took a deep breath, and said in a feigned matter-of-fact voice, "I know you from the Jewish Sports Club. Remember?"

She faced me with a tiny smile.

"I have never been to a sports club. Are you not confusing me with someone else?"

"I admit I am confused."

"Habitually?" she asked.

Walter explained that in order to get closer to the start of the queue, she needed to be his sister.

"So, what's your name, brother?" she asked.

And so it began. Her name was Rahli Feldman. It was a difficult time for a German Jew to woo a young lady, as so few places were accessible to non-Aryans. Rahli was the daughter of a half-Jewish father and a non-Jewish mother but, according to the law, she was of tainted blood. Simply taking a walk was not advisable for a young couple; one could be ordered to show identification papers at any time by police and SS. Walter lived in a rented room under the eye of a nosy landlady. A few weeks after their meeting, Rahli invited him to her home, to "meet my people." From Walter's own notes:

On Saturday, Rahli answered the door casually dressed. After the introduction to her parents, I entered the dining room. It was tastefully furnished. On the wall opposite hung a large photograph of one of the great beauties of Europe. I immediately recognized the film star Evelyn Hoelderlin.

"Your sister?"

Rahli nodded without an air of presumption, but her mother followed my admiring glances with unconcealed pride. Frau Feldman was in her early forties, still very attractive. Rahli's father, a tall and handsome man, was in his early sixties. He was a professional singer; baritone, I believe. As a half-Jew, his successful career had practically come to an end.

During the lunch, Herr Feldman suggested Rahli try dental technology; the family hoped to emigrate and such skill might be useful. Of course, Rahli agreed and soon began her studies in a nearby dental laboratory. For a few brief months, this handsome couple were so intensely enveloped in their passionate love the ugliness of the world outside disappeared for never-forgotten moments. Perhaps the danger of their outings, their days and nights in villages outside of the city, added to their ardor. They were treading forbidden ground. She was one-quarter Jewish, Walter a full Jew; how the authorities would react to their relationship was an unknown. Only in their imagination could they have a future together.

My brother gave Rahli a ring and brought her home to Winzig to enchant the family. They lied to one another, promising to visit soon again. But, Herr Feldman accepted a prestigious position in the Soviet Union. Walter did not describe their parting.

My brother began to carry his English student visa, a few family photos, and his passport in his pocket whenever he left his room. More and more members of his circle of friends were disappearing, some into exile, many into *Nacht und Nebel*, into Night and Fog. That phrase was the Gestapo's designation for individuals destined to vanish without a trace. One day, working in the dental lab, Walter received a phone call. The voice on the line did not identify itself. Speaking just above a whisper, it said: "You are now an *N und N*. Do not return to your apartment. Leave." Walter understood. *N und N, Nacht und Nebel*; he was intended to disappear.

He put down his tools down and left the building. A train took him to Bremen and Walter boarded the next ship to England. He had received one letter from Rahli, and it was in his pocket. She was studying to become a pediatrician in St. Petersburg.

Walter found work in England among the German dentists who had emigrated earlier. After the declaration of war, however, his situation changed again. The British government designated all people who had come to the island with a German passport to be enemy aliens. (This action resembled the later confinement of the Japanese by the United States, even Japanese who were US citizens.) The British government made no differentiation between the 2,000 genuine refugees and the 250 others who were possibly potential spies. Some immigrants were shipped to Canada, the unlucky ones to Australia. Unlucky indeed. The admiralty leased a ship, the *Dunera* and sent those no longer welcome in England to Camp Hay in Australia. Walter described the 57-day-long trip in the most withering terms; the crew stole everything of value from the passengers and treated them as convicted criminals; hygienic conditions aboard ship were beyond description.

Camp Hay was in the desert center of the continent. It became the place of confinement for 6,780 men women and children of Japanese, Italian, or German heritage. The German Jews immediately severed themselves from the so-called Aryans and organized themselves into a community. The guards were relieved to have this group govern itself. Within a few weeks, there were lecture series, soccer teams, musical entertainment, debates, and more. After nearly three years, the English government permitted men willing to join in the defense of England to return. Walter volunteered and survived the London Blitz. Nine hundred of the "*Dunera* boys" remained in Australia where they and their descendants enriched the culture of the continent.

Friedel, the youngest of my three brothers, was a special worry for my parents. He had contracted strep throat when he was thirteen, and the illness had damaged one of his heart valves. No country permitted people with medical problems to immigrate for fear they might become burdens of the state. Friedel, too, had left Winzig when public education became unbearable. When his former friends shunned him, he read the Karl May wild west stories over and over and did light chores for Papa. But Friedel was lonely and restless. On several occasions, he and I stood together behind a window curtain when a Hitler Youth troop passed our house singing the refrain of the new national anthem, the *Horst Wessel* Song: *Oh, when the blood of Jews spurts from our knives, then things go twice as well.* So, to get away, Friedel went to Breslau. He rented a room in a boarding house run by a Jewish landlady. Supposedly, he was apprenticed to a businessman but he actually spent most of his time at the movies.

Like the Steinhardts, the Moses family was also seeking refuge for their children. The eldest, my cousin Ruth, after passing her *Abitur*, found herself banned from any further education. Nonetheless, she found a reason to be happy. She met and fell in love with a suitable young man and we celebrated her engagement, soon followed by her marriage. Her wedding to Max Berns was the last time the extended family, even relatives from New York, gathered together. Margot and I, in keeping with tradition, recited a poem to honor the young couple. The wedding pictures show us sitting cross-legged in front of a large assemblage.

The newlyweds worked frantically to assemble the dozens of documents required by the German and American governments to emigrate and immigrate. But, the first member of the Moses family to leave the country turned out to be Ruth's younger brother (Margot's older brother) Josef. A relative in New York provided the required affidavit of support. He was 19 when he left early in 1938. As a youngster, he had helped in our bakery and this experience secured him a job baking bread in the Bronx, a borough of the city of New York. Four years later, he headed back to Europe, not as a stateless supplicant but a citizen wearing the uniform of an American soldier. Upon his safe return, the GI Bill of Rights enabled him to become a successful engineer.

Margot and I were the youngest children of both families, and letting us go must have been a heart-wrenching decision. At twelve years old, we had never been away from home. But, it was high time we left Winzig. We were the only Jewish children remaining in town and, although we were never beaten, we were openly cursed. Several of our classmates looked at us with pity and we found that more difficult to bear than spitefulness.

The Nazi system of education distorted the cultivation of the mind into an exaggerated emphasis on physical fitness: The Reich needed strong bodies to fill the ranks of future soldiers, and sturdy women to bear the next generation of soldiers. Every subject, from mathematics to literature to biology, was tainted by propaganda. Instruction became indoctrination.

Geography: Observe how our fatherland was squeezed into unnatural borders by our eternal enemies, the French and the English and their Jewish manipulators. German land was given away by the Versailles criminals who created the abomination of Poland and enriched France. Our Fuehrer has called the treaty a scrap of paper and he summons us to reclaim our lost lands. These we must safeguard with new conquests.

Mathematics: How many minutes and how many men will be required to shoot one thousand of our enemies using a machine gun of such-and-such caliber? How long will it take a mobilized army, proceeding at so many miles per hour, to march from Cologne to Paris? From Berlin to Warsaw?

The arts: Literature, painting, sculpture, and music all must serve to advance our national purpose. Culture for culture's sake, as expressions of individualism or rebellion, is meaningless and deserves to be banned. The object of true creativity is to display and glorify the Aryan genius. So-called modern art is a Jewish fraud.

Religion: Christ was an Aryan warrior. The concept of meek and gentle son of God taught in religious schools distorts the truth. Turning the other cheek displays weakness where strength should answer the insult. Now, let us learn more about the deities that were worshipped by our ancient forebears, Odin and Thor and Freya, and their ideals.

Biology: In nature the fittest survive; this applies to nations as well. Social Darwinism instructs us that the strong have an obligation and a right to rule the weak, whose purpose is nothing more than to serve the victors. Our Third Reich is based on that scientific principle. The Aryan race is the strongest, most creative, and most pure of all races of mankind. The very laws of natural selection made us superior. But even Aryans must be vigilant. The Jewish race is bent on destroying us, as it has destroyed other once-great civilizations.

Every minutia of German education was dictated from the ministry in Berlin. The traditional morning prayer, a brief appeal to God to help us have a productive day, was replaced by the stiff-armed Heil Hitler salute followed by words of gratitude to the Fuehrer for saving the nation. Recess changed from play time to a semi-military exercise as children marched in imitation of a military formation around and around the school yard. Children who needed glasses were ashamed to wear them, as poor eyesight was a sign of physical weakness. Also, glasses gave the wearer a studious appearance, not an attribute deemed desirable by the Hitler Youth. In many schools, discipline was enforced with a severity that bordered on cruelty. The cane was considered an adjunct to education. Humiliating reprimands, in some ways more hurtful than physical pain, were used to attack children who didn't measure up to Aryan standards of "fit to live in the Third Reich."

My eagerness to get away from Winzig was intensified by the loss of my dog. A smiling Mayor Lang had informed us a complaint had been lodged against Wambo, that the animal's barking disturbed the neighbors. We were given one week to dispose of him. If we did not comply, officer Urban was instructed to remove this public nuisance.

Wambo was my dog, a great Newfoundland with white and liver markings. He was gentle and infinitely patient as we dressed him, rode on his back, and put ribbons on his ears. He rarely barked, in fact, Papa complained Wambo was not much of a guard dog. But, he was my friend. I had kissed his slobbery face more often than that of any human. I told Wambo whatever was troubling me and knew that he understood. How was it possible that a word, indeed a lie, had the power to deprive me of my friend? Papa's assurance that he found a good home for Wambo did not dissolve the lump in my throat. On his last day with us, Papa put a collar and leash on Wambo, a new experience for the animal. He sensed something alarming was happening and began to howl. It was an eerie sound and, as I watched my father drag him away, I joined and we howled together. I, too, knew that something dreadful was taking place. Not only was I losing my friend, I was losing the confidence that within the walls of our house we were safe. Now I knew that even my strong and loving father could not protect us from the long reach of the Nazis.

The decision was made by our parents to send Margot me to Breslau. This provincial capital had a large Jewish presence, several synagogues and day schools. The leaders of the Reform congregation had opened the orphanage they supported, the *Waisenhaus,* to children from rural districts who had been ousted from their public schools. Thus, room and board was provided by the orphanage and education was available at the synagogue school. By the end of the summer of 1936, all the arrangements had been completed and Margot and I were ready for a new chapter in our lives. I was not frightened until my mother told me not to be frightened and hugged me long and hard. Uncle Jakob accompanied us on the bus and delivered us to the rather grim-looking gray stone building surrounded by a high wall, the *Waisenhaus.*

We were introduced to Frau Direktor, a stout lady with an imitation smile. Some years ago, she had been in charge of the orphaned girls, then married the administrator, a small, white-haired man whom we seldom saw and never heard. The couple had a cozy apartment on the ground floor. The second floor was divided between boys' and girls' quarters, each staffed with a professional social worker. Whether or not Frau Direktor had earned her own credentials or merely acted in her husband's name, we did not know. We did know, however, that she was the one in control.

The girls' section of the building, duplicated in the boys' wing, included a large day room decorated with a calendar but no other pictures. Chairs stood arranged around a long table, and some shelves provided for the few private possession permitted to us. That completed the furnishing. Margot and I were instructed by some of the older girls how to arrange our clothing in the narrow closets next to the dormitory on the third floor. Their advice: "Keep everything neat—Frau Direktor makes frequent inspections."

Some twenty of the younger girls slept on cots that lined dormitory walls; older girls, perhaps another ten, had a separate bedroom. Their "lights out" was later than ours. A row of washstands stood on iron legs in the center of both rooms, a small towel on a hook was changed every week. There was a bathroom with toilets and two tubs. On Friday afternoons, Frau Direktor supervised our five minutes per person in the bath. The water was changed several times and favorites were allowed to be first after a change.

When Margot and I arrived, supervision of the girls was in the hands of an efficient, yet gentle young woman who made life bearable for many of us. She was beautiful, kind, and immensely overworked. Every girl under her care carried a load of emotional baggage. Some cried often, others withdrew; a few vented their misery by striking out. We called her *Fraeulein* and with a hug, a word of encouragement, a smile, she held her motley group together. Frau Direktor disliked her and that made her more dear to us.

Fraeulein slept in her own quarters, and one night I woke up feeling sick and knocked on her door. She opened it just wide enough to step into the hall to ask me what was wrong. But, in that split second, I caught a glimpse of the handsome young man who was responsible for the boys' division. He was sitting on her bed. I told no one, not until this very moment. The knowledge that she, too, was flaunting the rules delighted me. When later I learned they had married and emigrated, I wished her happiness and embraced her in my thoughts.

I never quite adjusted to the pedagogy practiced at the orphanage— rules had to be followed without questions. Our first day set the tone for the next two years. Margot and I had joined the line-up of girls going downstairs to the dining hall for breakfast. As we passed the administrator's office, Frau Direktor came rushing out and slapped both of us in the face. Just like that. No reason given. We had been talking to each other, not loudly, quietly, and we did not know that talking was forbidden when going to meals. We looked at one another and swallowed hard. The corridors were but one of a number of no-talking zones. We stood in silence in line as we waited to for our food; and silence was expected while we ate. Boys sat one side, girls on the other, some fifty children having their meals without the murmur of voices. It was also unacceptable to leave any food on your plate. No excuses, you sat until the plate was empty; too bad if you threw up, then you had swallow that too. How a Jewish institution for children came to adopt this Prussian barrack mentality remains a mystery for me, as well as a distressing memory.

I became pretty effective in defying some of the most-hated dictates. When the food was particularly awful, I talked aloud and ignored the warning looks of the staff. My punishment? My full plate and I were sent from the dining room. Alone upstairs, I headed for the toilets. One flush, and the evidence was gone. In the evening, we were expected to fall asleep at lights out and the "no talking" rule applied again. I had traded one of my possessions for a flashlight and I read books under the bed covers. One day, a boy with lots of black, curly hair—his name was Heinie Schutz—slipped me a note in the dining hall. Thus began our exchange of secret messages. We rarely had the opportunity to speak to each other, but we enjoyed flouting the regulations that forbade such contact. Heinie emigrated to Argentina and we promised each other we would stay in touch. Everyone knew Frau Direktor read all our mail, but now Heinie was free to say whatever he liked. I received several letters, and I mailed my answers secretly but then heard no more from Heinie. Mail withheld? Destroyed? I'll never know.

Once a month, every child was weighed; the financial supporters of the orphanage judged their money well spent if the orphans gained weight according to a chart. I remained skinny, but found it useful to hide some small stones in my pocket before I stepped on the scale. I copied some of these defiance tactics from more experienced girls and other ploys I devised on my own. Margot joined me sometimes, but she had made more new friends than I, and her innate tendency to neatness and orderliness helped her to avoid conflicts.

The celebrations of Jewish holidays were a welcome relief from the dreariness of our routine: the food was better, the atmosphere lighter. Our favorite festival was Chanukah, eight days of candle-lighting, singing, and potato pancakes with applesauce. Part of the observance was an enactment by the children of some historic scenes connected to Chanukah. On that occasion, the audience included members of the executive committee governing the *Waisenhaus* as well as friends and relatives of the children. For some years, the production of the play had been a favorite project of Frau Direktor. One day, as winter approached, Fraeulein told me Frau Direktor wanted to see me. My reaction: "Now what did I do?"

But, instead of reproaches, I was invited into the living quarters. I sat on a real sofa and was asked if I'd like a banana. I did, and I relaxed and waited as Frau Direktor chattered about this and that. Finally, she came to the point: Would I help her with the Chanukah play? She had heard I could rhyme quite nicely and her plays had always been in verse and wouldn't it be lovely if we could create something splendid together? I would be welcome to come to her apartment in the evening, have some fruit, and we would work together on the play. If that was agreeable, I would be released from some other chore.

"I don't like darning the boys' socks on Sunday mornings," I suggested and she readily agreed to free me from that tedious duty.

For several weeks, we worked together. She chose the storyline, I crafted the rhyme. Our collaboration did not make me like her, but I did enjoy the treats and the heady notion that my knack with words might have some practical applications. The resulting play was a considerable success. The playbill mentioned all the performers and listed the Frau Direktor as author. Margot and some of my friends were incensed that my name had been left out. I was neither surprised nor unhappy.

They protested, "No one will know what you did."

I countered with, "But she knows. And I know."

Although I never felt at home during the two years my cousin and I spent in the orphanage, there were some compensations. My small acts of rebellion aside, I was comforted by weekly letters from my mother in Winzig and from my brother Walter in Berlin. Mutti wrote with a gentle affection she rarely expressed in person. I felt loved and comforted and homesick. Walter continued to urge me to study, and he introduced me to his heroes of the past, Thomas Jefferson and Thomas Paine, Goethe and Schiller among them. His own interests—history, philosophy, and literature—became my focus as well. I was grateful and proud that he took such caring interest in his little sister. But the foremost source of my willingness to behave tolerably well in the *Waisenhaus* was the opportunity to attend school.

Across the street from an imposing Reform synagogue stood a rectangular, sturdy building known as the *Schule am Anger*. Both boys and girls were admitted, but attended separate classrooms. The curriculum was modeled after a college preparatory program. Nearly all our teachers were proficient instructors; some had been dismissed from institutions of higher learning by the Nazi purge of Jews from public education. They knew their students faced problems that had no solution: unemployed fathers, money difficulties, endless discussions about emigration, friends and relatives leaving the country—or worse. No doubt, the faculty members were also concerned about their own futures. Nonetheless, they succeeded in instilling an atmosphere of normalcy into our classrooms.

Margot and my first day *am Anger* was not auspicious. Someone from the *Waisenhaus* had walked us to the school, arranged our registration, and left. Margot and I were handed our schedules, found the designated classroom, and knocked on the door.

"Enter" came a voice from within.

We walked in and the lady behind the desk asked, "Can I help you?"

"We are new students."

"But surely not in this class. The lower grades are on the first floor."

We handed her the registration forms. The teacher scanned them, then shook her head and with kindness said: "Pardon me, but you are quite right. We'll have to find you some seats."

When we looked at our classmates, we understood her confusion. The girls seated at their desks seemed to belong to a different world. They were taller, shapelier, and dressed in a fashion never seen in Winzig. Most wore traces of make-up, sported wristwatches, and had haircuts that originated in a salon, not a small-town barber shop. They wore shoes without laces, their stockings were not knitted by their mothers, and, oh, such slim skirts and open-necked blouses. Margot and I looked like leftovers from another place and time. We were smaller, still flat-chested, and our long-sleeved dresses buttoned to the neck. They were stylish teenagers of the city; we were children of the country. In addition to our lessons, Margot and I had to learn how to care about our appearance, how to make casual conversation, how to properly voice an opinion to an adult, and of, course, what was right and what was wrong about boys. We were never able to emulate such sophistication, but we watched and listened.

Academically, we proved our rightful placement in the class. Margot was a fine all-around student and excelled in math. I enjoyed a small triumph a couple of weeks after our enrollment. The subject was literature, and the assignment had been to read Knut Hamsun's classic *Hunger* and to write a critique of the book. The instructor had called on several students to read their essays, but she ignored my raised hand. I believe she wanted to save me embarrassment. But, when no one else volunteered, she had no choice but to call on me. I stood up and after the first few sentences felt my audience was attentive. When I stopped, there was a smattering of applause and praise from the teacher. I had secured my niche.

But the world outside could not be shut out. It entered the classroom no matter what the subject. Even here, we had to be careful not to voice any criticism of the Nazi regime; the walls were said to have ears. All of us were preoccupied with the uncertainties of our futures. Where would we end up? Which country—indeed, which continent? Every month, several girls would announce they were leaving Germany and the rest of us would look at them with envy, anxiety, and hope. Sporadically, the tension created by our insecurities resulted in tears or anger or sullenness. Most of our teachers were professionals who handled us with understanding and respect, and we responded. But poor Kantor who taught a Jewish religion class was the exception. The subject was of little to no interest to us, and his lack of authority made him our victim. We paid no attention, did no homework, and treated him shabbily. One day, some of the girls darkened the classroom and wove twine from desk to desk about an inch from the floor across the aisle that led to his desk. Kantor entered and we thought his stumbling and tumbling hilarious. He must have really needed that job, because he never reported us. In a day or two, we were contrite. We had shamed him, and that was wrong. We did behave a little better, but, poor man, this was not the time to instruct us on the power and mercy of the Almighty.

I kept a diary between 1935 and 1939, and I have often wished I could still refer to it. At times I am uncertain whether I recall my emotions and reactions accurately, but there are some scenes that are very clear in my mind. One of those was my encounter with Gisela.

The last school bell had rung and Margot and I were on our way to the orphanage when I realized I had forgotten a book. I ran back to the classroom. One girl was still at her desk, her face in her hands, sobbing in staccato bursts. It was Gisela, a girl I admired greatly and envied frequently—always from afar; we had never had a conversation. I stopped in the doorway, confused. I thought: "Why is she crying? She has everything: her father is a dentist, she is tall and good-looking with a great figure and stylish clothes. If I had what she has, I cannot imagine why I would cry. Just look at that watch with the leather strap! At the belt with nail heads! Silk stockings! What else could she possibly want?"

I hesitated, wondering what to do. Gisela had not noticed me. I gathered my courage and sat down on the chair next to her.

"Gisela, can I do anything?"

She did not look up but shook her head.

"Gisela, what's wrong?"

Without lifting her head she said, "My father was arrested this afternoon. Gestapo."

I was stunned. I could think of nothing to console her. Then, I felt ashamed. "Papa," I thought, "My wonderful Papa, what would we do without you? Poor Gisela, she would give up everything to have her father home."

Gisela was weeping more quietly. I wanted to stroke her hair, but did not; perhaps she would not welcome my touch. I stayed a few minutes longer and then quietly left, closing the door gently, as one does when leaving a hospital room.

CHAPTER 5

PAPA SAID: 'I WISH I HAD ASKED HIS NAME'

Margot and I completed the final grade offered in Breslau's *Schule am Anger* in the spring of 1937. We left the *Waisenhaus* with relief and spent a rather joyless and friendless summer at home. Perhaps some of our former Winzig schoolmates may have wished to see us but feared taunts from members of the Hitler Youth. We did not expect such courage from our erstwhile comrades and rarely ventured into town. Our most pressing concern was the immediate future. We were fifteen years old. What could we do? Where could we go? One of the several Jewish self-help institutions offered a temporary solution; the *Paula Ollendorf Haushaltungsschule*. This facility was designed to turn Jewish girls into accomplished homemakers: good wives and intelligent mothers. Besides cooking, cleaning, ironing, some sewing, child care, and budgeting, several academic classes were available—the latter for a fee; a fee the Moses and Steinhardt families could not afford. Never mind, it was important to get us out of Winzig, to move us into the company of Jewish students and teachers. And so we cousins returned to the Silesian capital and joined fifty or sixty other teenaged girls at the school. We were housed in a modern building—shared bedrooms but not a dormitory—worked in kitchens with modern appliances, and attended classes. Though supervised, we were not unduly controlled, and we liked our instructors. It was not necessary to warn us not to walk around the neighborhood and never to leave the building without a buddy.

Our courses promoted the aims of the school's founders with practical and theoretical lessons. A weeklong workshop on the Montessori method of child rearing was given at a kindergarten for Jewish children—that was my favorite class. This might indeed have been a valuable and satisfying phase in our lives had it been possible to separate ourselves from the intensifying persecution by the Nazi government. All of us, including our teachers, were preoccupied by our anxieties. Instead of talking about parties, we discussed immigration quotas; instead of trying new hairstyles, we wondered what was happening to our families; instead of reading fashion magazines, we worried about the next restrictive, anti-Semitic decree. We shared our fears and wiped away some bittersweet tears each time a classmate packed her bags to restart life in another country.

At the end of one year, Margot took leave from the *Haushaltungsschule* to take a job as a *Haustochter* in Berlin. *Haustochter* translates literally to "daughter of the house," but that was a euphemism. The Jewish middle class customarily had employed German maids but the Nuremberg Laws of 1935 had virtually banned that practice. No matter, the deteriorating income of the Jewish population could no longer support such a luxury. In response to this dilemma, homeowners supplemented their income by renting their spare rooms to the growing number of dispossessed Jews. Obviously, this increased the burdens of the woman of the house and the answer to that problem was the *Haustochter.*

Advertisements in Jewish newspapers brought potential employers and their ersatz daughters together. The work was described as light; the wages paid were less than light. Girls from rural areas were favored, reputed to be unspoiled and good workers. For young Jewish women, the incentive to leave their rural homes was twofold: one, they were lonely, and, two, they hoped to study the language of the country to which they expected to emigrate. Unemployed teachers came to the residence and offered weekly lessons for a few Marks. So, while waiting for that ship to come and take them into better world, some girls went to the city. Often, they found themselves worked as if they were adults but treated as if they were children.

In 1938, even though Margot had gone to Berlin, I returned to the *Haushaltungsschule*, expecting to complete one more year. But, within a few months all Jewish institutions were shut down. The nationwide pogrom *Krystallnacht* (Crystal Night) was the beginning of the end of German Jewish life. I was in Breslau during the days of arson, looting, rioting, and arrests, yet I admit to a total inability to recall the event. I do remember one of the teachers, Fraeulein Schwartz, announcing in a strangely shaky voice that the closing of the school was imminent; we all must leave as quickly as possible. To go where? I have no recollection of the next several days. How did I get home? Did I take the bus? A train? Did I first go to relatives living in Breslau? I simply do not know. The phone lines of Jewish customers had been disconnected. My mother was returning from a trip to Berlin with her niece Ruth and Ruth's husband Max. Did I know about their traumatic journey? All my efforts to reconstruct the days during and immediately following the Night of the Broken Glass have been futile, wiped away without a trace.[1]

The history of the *Kristallnacht* is familiar to students of the Third Reich and in this context the briefest review will suffice.

In October of 1938, the Nazi government decreed the expulsion of all Jews born in Poland, including those who had attained German citizenship. The Gestapo herded some 7,000 men, women, and children into trains that headed eastward. The Polish authorities, however, refused to admit them and ordered the Jews away from Polish soil. So, the families trekked back into the no-man's land between the borders. Their expulsion had been ordered without any notice, so food and money ran out very quickly. Worldwide Jewish organizations applied pressure and payment to persuade the Polish government to accept these suddenly homeless and stateless refugees. Among these people were the parents and sister of seventeen-year-old Hershel Grynspan, who was studying in Paris. A postcard from his sister confirmed that she and his mother and father were among the refugees. He became frantic, managed to obtain a revolver, and went to the German embassy in Paris to exact revenge. There, he shot the third secretary, Ernst vom Rath. The wounded official lingered for a day and died on November 9.

That same week, the Nazi hierarchy had gathered in Munich to celebrate the anniversary of an earlier and unsuccessful attempt to overthrow the Bavarian government. When news of the shooting reached the assembled "old fighters," three of the nation's most powerful men—Hermann Goering, Josef Goebbels, and Heinrich Himmler—decided, with Hitler's consent, to use the assassination "to teach the Jews a lesson." Emigration had, in their view, been too slow, and a nationwide pogrom would speed the Jewish exodus.

The "lesson" consisted of the immediate arrest and incarceration of all Jewish males between the ages of sixteen and sixty, as well as the destruction of all Jewish communal institutions and businesses. The prisoners, estimated at 30,000, were shipped to the nearest concentration camps. The Nazis had begun to build and use these massive penal compounds from the beginning of their reign, supposedly for the re-educating of political prisoners. That façade was dropped; now, the crime was being Jewish, the method of instruction was terror. The objective was to make the nation *Judenrein.*

From this moment, the rule of law no longer applied to the Jewish population. The state itself had become the instrument of lawlessness. Well-prepared, well-organized Nazi Party enforcement agencies—such as the SA, SS, and Gestapo—together with the police and the courts created a lethal combination that criminalized the mere existence of non-Aryans. The fact that the Night of the Broken Glass did not enrage the German people despite its nationwide destruction and lawlessness, was a frightening wake-up call for German and Austrian Jewry. Some Gentiles regretted the disorder, some looked, most looked away. There was not much visible looting, useable goods strewed about were quickly picked up and hidden. Firefighters idled by their trucks as buildings owned by Jews burned, but, as instructed, doused only neighboring structures belonging to non-Jews. Members of the regular police obeyed orders not to interfere in the chaos.

Our family fared better than most during Crystal Night. My brother Walter was in England; Dicker, now Jup, in Holland; and Friedel lived in his Jewish boardinghouse in Breslau. He was warned to disappear by a Christian friend, and he spent a night and day in a Catholic cemetery. After dark, cold and hungry, he made his way back to his room. His landlady greeted him with tears and told him he had evaded arrest by a few hours. He was seventeen. Although Friedel, the youngest of my three brothers, looked sturdy and was quite handsome, his clogged heart valve impaired his stamina. Had he been arrested and imprisoned, he might not have survived. So, on the night of November 10, he shakily climbed up to his attic room, but he found his bed occupied. To his delighted amazement, two ladies were asleep between his rarely changed sheets—his mother and his cousin Ruth. What brought the two women to Friedel's rather humble lodgings? Their story began in Berlin.

Ruth and her husband Max had expected to leave for the United States in a few days. The American consulate had issued their visas and, on November 9, they boarded a train to say goodbye to Ruth's parents. My mother had been visiting other emigrating relatives in Berlin and she joined the young couple on their way to Winzig. Their journey turned into a nightmare. From the windows of their railroad compartment, they saw fires all along their route. Train stops were particularly harrowing; they witnessed scenes of brutality against Jewish travelers as men were beaten and separated from their screaming families. Clearly, some anti-Jewish campaign was in progress, but they had no idea of its cause or extent. In Breslau, they needed to change trains to get to Winzig. As they hurried to the proper platform, they were stopped. Max was the target of a pair of SS men.

"Jew?"

"Yes, sir."

"You are under arrest."

"But why?'

No answer. The troopers seized Max by his elbows and tried to pull him away from the women. Ruth began to scream. She threw herself at her husband. With her right fist she beat his chest, her left arm circled his neck. The Nazis began to hit Max with their batons, but Ruth held on for another few seconds. Then she let him go and watched as he was led from sight. Mutti, shaken but composed, said:

"There was no way you could have stopped them. You were very brave to try."

Ruth replied: "I knew that. It's our papers I wanted: our passports, tickets, everything was in the breast pocket of Max's coat—now they are in my muff. Without them, we wouldn't have a chance. With them, the Nazis might let him go. They want to get rid of us, so here is proof that we were about to leave."

Her aunt shook her head in admiration and called her *Pudelchen*, (little poodle), a favorite nickname for her curly-haired niece.

The two women hurried from the station, uncertain what to do next. The train for Winzig had left and they were exhausted. My mother remembered that Friedel had a room near the station. The landlady welcomed them and offered them a cup of tea, which was gratefully accepted. Upstairs, they took off their shoes and, shivering with anxiety and fatigue, collapsed into Friedel's bed in the attic room.

The following day, Ruth began the seemingly impossible task of freeing her husband. She waited on more lines than she could remember and was sent from agency to agency, rebuffed and ridiculed. But, she persevered. The proof that she and her husband she were about to leave the fatherland won Max an early release and, within a few weeks, they sailed for the United States.

Friedel decided to remain in Breslau, where he had friends. A second Gestapo raid on the boardinghouse seemed unlikely. But Mutti was desperate to go home. She had seen the chaos, the arson, and the foot-high broken glass on the sidewalks, and was frantic to learn where I was and what had happened in Winzig. Not only had telephones of Jewish subscribers been disconnected, there were also rumors that public call boxes were monitored by the government. She paced the floor until she could wait no longer. Mutti kissed Friedel and her *Pudelchen* and ventured into the street, still heavy with smoke. She reached home later that day, but she could never recall just how she got there; another example of selective amnesia related to stressful traveling. Her sister Augusta and her sister-in-law Anna greeted her with tears of joy. The news that Ruth was safe but Max arrested was accepted with predictably mixed emotions. Mutti was not surprised to learn the men of the house had been taken; she was thankful the house was intact. Ugly curses had been smeared with tar on walls and windows; she would wash them away, although one of the slogans made her hands fly to her heart: *Jude verrecke* (Jew, die in filth).

True to his word, Hugo Kliem did not abandon his friends. He came every evening and he offered to shop in town if the women needed anything. Before dawn and again after dusk, he climbed through the hole he had cut into the back fence that separated our properties and took care of our animals. He milked the cows, fed the horses, and cleaned their stalls. He did these chores without being asked, and he would not allow my mother to thank him.

Aunts Anna and Augusta and my Mutti decided to sleep, or try to sleep, in the same room. During the night, just before dawn, my Aunt

Anna heard a rattle against the bedroom window. Then another. My mother and her sister woke up. Aunt Augusta whispered:

"They're back. The Nazis are back."

Aunt Anna shook her head, "They wouldn't throw gravel, they'd throw stones."

Mutti peered through the curtain and in the moonlight she recognized my father. The three women rushed to the stairs, but my mother was not the one to open the door—she had fainted on the landing. Anna stepped outside, greeted her brother, then she looked to the right, looked to the left, then looked directly at Papa. He shook his head and lifted his palms in a gesture of futility. She understood: *I do not know where Jakob and Adolph are; I am alone.* My mother got to her feet and wept in her husband's arms. Although too exhausted to eat, Papa checked on the livestock in the barn and found everything in good order. He sat down and promptly fell asleep; the story of his exploits had to wait until morning.

Many years later, I asked my father to write down his Crystal Night recollections; I have them, inked in his feathery Gothic script. But, over the years, he repeated his story many times, I can recall it without reservations:

> I will begin from the beginning. It must have been close to eight o'clock when I heard banging on the front door. Not knocking, banging. With Jakob and Adolph behind me, I let two men in civilian clothing into the house. Gestapo, they said. One of them had a list and he asked our names. Then, he said we were under arrest and ordered us to get into the car parked on the curb. We were never told why we were arrested. I had taken off my work shoes and was wearing a pair of old slippers. So, I asked for permission to put on my shoes. The older one, he seemed to be in charge, he didn't answer in words, just put his hand on his revolver, a gesture clearer than language.
>
> That's how I came to be arrested in my slippers.

Our first stop was the basement room of our town hall. The only other Jewish man who still remained in Winzig, Herr Arnholtz, was already there. We were locked in, bars on the windows. We stood around for several hours. All this time no one told us anything. Before dawn, a police car came and took us to Wohlau; probably because the county seat has a large jail. It was a busy night there, maybe a hundred Jewish men questioned and frisked. The SS trooper who searched us shouted: "Anyone found with a weapon will be executed at once." We were taken to a cell and told to undress. Although we were hungry, we could not eat the rotting potatoes and shriveled herring thrown at us.

On the next afternoon, the cells were opened. We lined up, were counted, pushed into trucks, and driven to Breslau. What we saw there stopped us from speaking. Passing through Jewish neighborhoods, we saw many fires, some buildings already in ashes. Police and firemen were rushing around in their vehicles, but doing nothing to stop the destruction. We saw Nazi thugs throwing furniture, pictures, bedding, dishes, even clothing, out of windows. Breslau's great Reform Synagogue was a heap of rubble. Later, we heard it would not burn, so it was dynamited. Some sights are hard to describe, like wine from a liquor flowing down the street and feathers from a bedding store floating, turning red and then disappearing.

"Sodom and Gomorrah," I thought.

Jakob and I had no idea what happened to our children and wives. That was the hardest to bear. We knew that Rosa [Mutti] and Ruth and Max were on a train, but nothing more. Had Friedel, too, been arrested? Among the prisoners on our truck were youngsters his age. Margot was in Berlin, Rita in school in Breslau. Were they all right? We saw men clubbed, but not women, that gave us a glimmer of hope.

No one spoke about his fears, but all of us were scared. Would we be shot? Imprisoned? God forbid, sent to a KZ [concentration camp]? Maybe pushed across some border? Anything was possible; this was a Germany we did not recognize.

Did I mention the tons upon tons of broken glass that covered sidewalks, even some streets? At first I thought it was ice. The smashed storefronts and window panes actually sparkled, and they crunched underfoot.

It was evening when we arrived at Breslau's police headquarters. There, we were ordered to jump from the truck and run between two rows of Blackshirts[2] into the yard. The Nazis used their clubs as we passed, yelling curses and *"Schnell, schnell"* (quickly, quickly). Some of the men were beaten badly and were bleeding; I was lucky, just a lump on my arm.

The yard was already packed with many hundreds, maybe thousands of men. And still more kept coming. Yet, it was quiet. We spoke little, only in whispers. That when I first heard the name Grynspan[3]. In the crowd I lost the other Winzigers. I searched as best I could but they were swallowed up. It was like trying to a find a certain bee in a whole swarm. Among all those men, I was alone. That was a bad moment for me, a really bad moment.

We were confined in a large compound, perhaps half a hectare [one hectare is roughly 2.5 acres]. I think all that space was the training ground for mounted police. Now it was packed with Silesian Jews. A high wall, maybe ten feet or more, surrounded us on three sides, and on the fourth stood the police building .There were watchtowers and guards with rifles patrolling on the top of the walls. Searchlights swept over us every few seconds. I moved around as best I could, still looking for Jakob or Adolph, when I noticed the SS were lining up queues of prisoners near the entrance of the headquarters, Small groups were sent into the building. I saw them go in but no one came out. A bad sign.

It was getting cold. Remember, I only had my slippers, no shoes. My toes were getting numb. Frostbite? Amputations? If I survived whatever lay ahead and could not walk, what good would I be? A useless burden, God forbid. I needed to find something to lean on so I could rub my feet. I headed to the nearest wall, to a spot the searchlights missed. As I moved along the bricks, I suddenly touched wood. Groping with my hands, I touched iron hinges. I had stumbled onto a door. I pressed the handle and *Gott im Himmel* [God in heaven] it opened.

Quickly, I stepped inside—a boiler room or coal storage space from the smell of it. A bit of light came through the bottom of a door behind me and I could make out a small staircase. I sat down and rubbed my feet. First, they hurt. Then, I felt a blessed tingle. How long did I sit there? I have no idea. Long enough to start thinking, how could I get home? What could I do or say to get released? As I warmed up, I considered all sorts of schemes, some pretty foolish. But then, I had a thought and in the next few minutes it became a plan. I stood up and straightened my clothes and my back.

Five steps up and I was in a long and busy hallway. Uniformed and plain-clothed officials were hurrying here and there, ignoring me. Offices lined both sides of the corridor, their doors were open. I saw men like me standing before the desks of officials. I thought they were being registered or questioned. I wanted to talk to one of these officials, but to which one? Quickly, I looked around, searching for someone older, not in Nazi uniform. Then, I spotted one. He wore glasses, he was perhaps my age, around fifty.

I crossed the room and waited for him to notice me. A minute went by. He never raised his head, even when he cursed me. Selecting him was a mistake. He called me a *Schweinehund* and other words I won't repeat.

I figured I had nothing to lose, and said: "Sir, please. I am a farmer and have several fresh-milking cows. If I am not home to take care of them, they will get sick and die. Most respectfully, I request you release me to take care of the animals."

The man began to shout, "Get out, get out, you filthy Jew."

I turned and left but used a different door, one across the room. Why? I don't know.

Now I was in a wide, busy hallway, men in uniforms and civilians rushing from one place to another. At the far end I saw an exit sign. I walked quickly, trying to look like a man on an errand. If I seemed confused or aimless, my unshaved face and slippers would land me back in the yard. Suddenly, an SS man came up from behind me and yelled for me to stop. I stopped. The Blackshirt, a big fellow, half dragged, half carried a pitiful invalid, an obviously sick, old Jew. I expected the Nazi's fist in my face, but instead he asked: "You leaving?"

"Yes, sir."

"Here, take this one out with you."

With that, he threw that poor old fellow toward me. I grabbed hold of him before he fell, His legs seemed useless, so I held him up as we walked.

I could barely hear him when he whispered: "I'm unfit to travel. That's why they let me go. You don't look unfit."

"Haven't been released. Trying to find a way out of here."

"No exemption card? Oh my! You won't make it."

We were getting closer to the exit and the two policemen guarding it.

My new friend asked: "Children?"

Strange question, I thought, but I told him, "Four."

"I don't; no wife no kids. But you, you're needed. Here, take my card, get yourself home. Go ahead."

"Can't do that."

At this point we were just a few meters from the exit.

The old man spoke again, but his voice was so weak I could barely hear him:

"Let's try to get out together. Two on one ticket. Are you game?"

I held my breath, unable to speak, closed my eyes for a second, then nodded. We were at the great double doors. My wreck of an invalid held up the proof of his release. A mere glance from one of the guards and we kept going. Never will I forget the words of one of the policemen, "Lucky dogs." The two sentries posted outside at the top of the stairs leading to the street never asked for any papers.

Quickly, we crossed the road and headed for a dark alley. My new friend seemed to feel much better as we hurried along, my burden was getting lighter. He no longer clutched at me, but actually kept pace with me as we sought shelter in a doorway. When I got a good look at him, even in the dim light, I could not believe my eyes. Was this the same man? He was probably younger than I. And now he was laughing! I was stunned, and hardly found the words to ask:

"Who are you?"

"If you lived in Breslau and went to the theater, you certainly would know me. I am an actor. Tonight, I played my best role. And to think, you were my only audience."

I must have said *Donnerwetter* [thunder-weather, an idiom expressing amazement] ten times. I tried to thank him, but he would not allow it. Did I have some place I could go until it was safe to go home, he asked. I told him that my wife's cousin lived not far, yes, I could find my way.

"But what about you?" I asked him.

"Ah, this my city, I have many friends to help me."

And so we shook hands and I watched him stride away.

I wish I had asked his name.

My father found cousin Herta's apartment; her husband, too, had been arrested. Papa ate, washed, and slept a few hours. In the evening, he shaved, put on a pair of too-tight shoes belonging to Herta's husband, borrowed some money, and went to the train station. Some fires were still burning, but the previous night's chaos had run its course. There was no direct train to Winzig until the next day, so he bought a ticket to Steinau, the closest stop. From there, Papa planned to walk, about three or four hours, and arrive home before sun-up.

On the train, he hid his face behind a newspaper but no one questioned him. When he arrived in Steinau, a familiar voice called him, "Herr Steinhardt, Herr Steinhardt, it's me, Ernst. I am a taxi driver now. Quick. Get in." Another minor miracle: Ernst had been Papa's driver when we had a car. They reached Winzig without incident. Papa had no money with him and asked Ernst to wait a few minutes, and he would get the fare. Ernst replied:

"Please, don't pay me. Today, I am ashamed to be a German, and if you let me do this favor for you, I will feel a little better. And, no, you don't have to warn me, I never saw you."

Papa gratefully breathed a prayer. The house was undamaged, and he knew the women would choose to sleep together in the front bedroom. He bent down and gathered a handful of gravel.

At five o'clock in the morning, he was in the barn when Hugo Kliem arrived. The men slapped one another on the back and, in answer to Hugo's question, my father told him he had been sent home to care for the animals. That story was soon making the rounds in Winzig. During the following weeks, my uncles returned from Buchenwald. They looked haggard, thin, and Jakob had lost some teeth. They would not talk of their experiences in the concentration camp except to say their release was predicated on signing a promise to emigrate as soon as possible. Both men had searched for Papa in the camp and finally decided he must have been killed. His survival seemed miraculous. With very few omissions, all adult Jewish men had been incarcerated. The official designation was "protective custody to save them from the righteous wrath of the German people over the murder of Third Secretary vom Rath." About 100 were killed during the chaotic first day and night. Depending on location, they were shipped to the nearest concentration camp: Dachau in the south, Sachsenhausen in northern Germany, and, for most of Prussia, Buchenwald. Between 800 and 1,000 prisoners died during their incarceration; the number of suicides ran high, but only estimates are available.

Was this the beginning of the Holocaust? The fact that the prisoners were not systematically murdered but were permitted to return has persuaded scholars *Kristallnacht* may have been a test to evaluate the world's reaction. The response of most foreign governments to this return to medievalism was expressed in protests, some quite vigorous, even the recall of some ambassadors, but such reproaches were considered acceptable by the Nazi regime. Hitler had his answer; in the judgment of the world the Jews were expendable, he was free to do as he pleased with those who could not or would not emigrate.

For most German and Austrian Jews, the search for a haven became frantic. The German government chose to hold all Jews responsible for or a crime committed by one Jew. This concept of collective guilt and collective punishment became standard procedure during the Holocaust. It was obvious the *Kristallnacht* pogrom had been carried out under orders from Nazi leadership, and the claim that the Jews themselves were responsible for the destruction of their institutions and the arrests was so absurd, it was ludicrous. A one billion Mark penalty was imposed for "inciting" the pogrom at the very moment the Jewish community needed funds for self-help.

The method of payment for this enormous sum included surrendering all items of value. My father carted a large box to city hall. Inside was our silver samovar, the candlesticks, jewelry, and furs. Bank accounts came under the control of the state; we were permitted to withdraw three hundred Marks each month of our own money. The so-called Aryanization of property was accelerated. This permitted Aryans to buy up Jewish properties for a small percent of their value. Our buildings and garden, previously appraised at 100,000 Marks, was forced into sale at 30,000 Marks. Because the new owner was unable to take immediate possession of his bargain, he rented it back to us and we were able to remain in our house. Goering, the most avaricious of the Fuehrer's intimates, called the heads of insurance companies into his office. He informed them that payment on insured losses was expected, but the money was not to be disbursed among the policyholders, it belonged to the state. The businesses, factories, professional offices, and communal institutions destroyed on Crystal Night were closed, permanently. To deal with all of the Jewish communities in the country as a single entity, prominent Jews were appointed and held responsible for compliance of all further instructions of the regime. This decision foreshadowed the Jewish Councils, the *Judenraete*, of the ghettos to come.

Following the massive pogrom, the number of new laws restricting, demeaning, pauperizing, isolating, and dehumanizing the Jews would fill many pages. Jews could not leave their domiciles without a *Kennkarte*, an identity card which recorded their fingerprints. Jewish females had to add "Sara" as their middle name, while Jewish males had to add Israel. Jews could own no pets, could only shop at certain hours on certain days, had to observe a curfew, and on and on.

But this was in the future. A more immediate concern was my inability to return to Breslau from Winzig. Jewish educational institutions had been shut down, and German schools were for Aryans only. I must have been a sorry sight, moping around the house. What to do with a fifteen-year-old girl? The solution of becoming a *Haustochter* seemed better than staying home. Rather halfheartedly, I took the train to Berlin to become a maid in the home of people I did not know.

The lady of the house was tall and stern, her husband short and nearly silent. Their apartment was large, and they had rented three rooms. I was expected to keep the entire flat neat and clean, turn all the mattresses once a week, do dishes, help in the kitchen, and hand-wash "personals." Frau Loewenthal was an exacting employer; her reprimands included: "There are stains on the kitchen towel [which she doled out once a week] that shows you don't wash the dishes properly." I had to eat my meals with the couple and Frau Loewenthal would never give me enough to eat. I was always hungry. She kept a box of cornflakes under lock and key, along with all other edibles. When I took my weekly bath, I was allowed no more than three centimeters of water. My room was a converted closet, and I slept on a fold-up cot. There was no lock on my door and one evening I saw the handle turn, very slowly and quietly. I opened the door and there stood Herr Loewenthal, mumbling some excuse. After that, I secured my privacy by moving my cot to block the entrance. An instructor in English came once a week, but I was usually too tired to pay proper attention.

After two or three months, I developed pains in my side and I visited a doctor. His prescription, "Go home. At once. You are greatly under-nourished. Your kidneys have lost their fatty casements, and you need food and rest."

The lady of the house cried when she heard I had to leave, claiming I was as dear to her as a daughter. My mother's reaction when I walked into the house in Winzig was to blame herself for allowing me to work in Berlin. She threw her hands up and wailed, "God in heaven, what have I done to you?"

Under Mutti's care, I was better in a few weeks. Papa kept me busy filling out the many forms required for our anticipated emigration. Our lives were in a holding pattern, but, after my stint as a *Haustochter*, I was glad to be home.

Both my mother and father had siblings who had emigrated to the United States as teenagers and who sent us the required affidavits that obligated them to support us if necessary. Even with the assurance we would not become burdens of the state, the waiting period for emigration to the United States was four to five years. Immigration laws favored western Europeans and the State Department had permitted its prejudices to influence the law. My parents and brother Friedel were placed on the much-smaller Polish quota because they had been born in the German province of Posen, which became part of Poland after the Great War. Only I was classified as a native of Germany. By a stroke of the pen, uncounted numbers of applicants were maneuvered out of the more liberal German allotment into the highly restricted Polish quota. This suited the head of the immigration desk of the US State Department, the anti-Semitic Breckenridge Long, who instructed his consuls to "delay, delay, delay" the release of visas.

The delay in Washington resulted in the death of many tens of thousands, but a loophole in the system escaped the notice of the bigots. Breckenridge Long tried to keep my family out, but a truly great American allowed us to enter: none other than Abraham Lincoln. In 1862, President Lincoln signed the Homestead Acts which enabled farmers to come and settle the open expanse of the Northwest Territories. These laws were never repealed, and the farmer-friendly legislation made the Steinhardts eligible for visas outside the quota system.

Our application to farm in the United States was given preferred attention by the consulate staff in Berlin. But, a special requirement had to be met to assure the US Consul that, indeed, our request was based on practical evidence. So, my father and Friedel received a letter. They were requested to come to the American Consulate in Berlin to take a test that would verify (or not) their claim to be admitted to the United States as modern pioneers. What sort of test? There was lots of speculation, but no one knew. Father and son went off to keep the appointment.

In Berlin, the two Steinhardts we taken into separate rooms. Both were shown trays that had been partitioned into small sections, each of which was filled with a handful of kernels.

"Identify these," the staff member said.

Papa later said he thought it took him five seconds to identify the seeds; Friedel admitted to a second or two longer: wheat, rye, oats, barley, alfalfa, etc. Without hesitation, both named all the grains correctly. A congratulatory handshake followed, and then the promise that, upon passing the medical examination and submission of our passports, the Steinhardt family would be granted that elusive, life-giving stamp, our visas to the United States. My mother and I were automatically part of the package. When my father and brother returned, we felt like dancing. But not for long, there was yet another hurdle to be jumped: Friedel's heart condition. Certificates from a German doctor were not acceptable. The examination must take place at the Consulate, performed by an American physician. When my parents thought I was asleep, I heard their whispers:

"What do we do if Friedel is rejected?"

"You go with Rita I'll stay."

"No. I'll stay, you go."

Then, I heard my mother sigh and then silence.

Late one evening, Mutti went out. That was unusual.

"Where is she going?"

Papa said Mutti had gone to talk to Dr. Loele. In our minds, there was God, then next to him stood Dr. Loele. Never a Nazi, he had continued to look after our family, making his visits to our house at night.

"Is Mutti sick?"

"No, she wants to ask him something."

I was puzzled but my father's face was closed to further questions.

Not until the day we traveled to Berlin to undergo the physical exam did I learn the purpose of Mutti's call on Dr. Loele. Just before Friedel went to see the doctor, she handed him two tiny pills and told him to place them under his tongue.

"Dr. Loele's order," she explained. "It's to make your heart sound better."

While my brother was in the examination room, my father paced, Mutti shredded her handkerchief, and I had to remind myself to breathe. When the door opened and he stood there smiling, we all went limp from the release of our tension.

We will never know if the American doctor heard the murmur and decided to allow this handsome young man to remain with his family, or if the nitroglycerin actually masked the symptom. We thanked the good Lord for his blessings: We would go to the United States together.

But not so fast, Herr Steinhardt. The required passports had to be issued by the local authority, and that meant Mayor Lang. Day after day Papa went to city hall to request them, day after day Mayor Lang laughed, and told him to return tomorrow, perhaps then.... Meanwhile, the first of September came and went. We watched as the German army rolled toward the Polish border. This was the Blitzkrieg army, mobile to an unprecedented degree, moving eastward in trucks, motorcycles, and tanks. Even their mess kitchens traveled on wheels. These soldiers were not given a jubilant send-off by the onlookers, no hurrahs, no flowers and few waves or smiles.

"This is nothing like the fervor of 1914," Hugo Kliem commented.

Winzigers generally accepted the quick surrender of Poland with relief rather than joy. Now, they expected a quick end to the war. England and France sending soldiers to die for Polskis? Not likely. But, they were mistaken. The months between the end of the Polish campaign and the spring of 1940 is often referred to as the *Sitzkrieg*—the sitting-down war—because no military action took place. The invasions of France, Holland, Belgium, Norway, and Denmark began on May 10, and the occupation of their port cities closed the main escape route for fleeing Jews.

But, by that time, my family had already left. Why were we so fortunate to escape the fate of the six million Jews who perished? Philosophically, I have no answer; but, practically, I am certain my father's saved us by his quick response to a letter he received in mid-December 1939. A member of the American consul's staff inquired why we had not come for our visas, had we made other arrangements?

After a few *Donnerwetters*, Papa stated he would immediately go to Berlin and explain the cause of our dilemma: that Mayor Lang was on a personal vendetta against him. He would affirm that we were most eager to go to America. Mutti wondered how one got an appointment with the Consul.

"Never mind," Papa said, "just pack up a dozen eggs, and a pound of butter. I'll go kill a chicken and a goose. Put it all into a suitcase, and I'll find a way."

Food rationing had made such delicacies more precious than money. My father arrived at the consulate early in the morning and the eggs were a gift for the guard at the gate. This guard sent him on to a secretary who loved the butter. The secretary referred him to an aide, and, by the time the chicken and the goose had been gratefully received, Papa was in the office of Consul Raymond Geist. Papa explained how Winzig's mayor was the cat and he, Papa, the mouse, and that Papa hoped with all his heart to make a new life in America. The consul did not interrupt, but he seemed furious. He rang for a stenographer and, in my father's presence, dictated a telegram to Mayor Lang. It stated:

It has come to my attention that you are withholding the passports of Heymann, Rosa, Siegfried, and Rita Steinhardt. By this action you are opposing the policy of your own government, which is urging the emigration of its Jewish citizens. Unless the above mentioned family is issued their passports immediately, I will feel it to be my duty to notify the German authorities of your obstruction of their policies.

On the day following Papa's return, he went to city hall and on the counter were four passports. Mayor Lang was nowhere in sight. But, in his rush, the town clerk forgot to mark them all with the required "J," the symbol that the bearer was Jewish. This oversight would become the source of difficulties later. We had been half-packed for many weeks. Now, as required by law, Patrolman Urban came to supervise the sealing of our trunk and final packing of suitcases. He drank quite a bit of Papa's Schnapps and dozed in his chair. Still, I tore up, page by page, the diary I had kept over the last four years. By decree, it was forbidden to take any written or printed matter out of the country. Despite the snoring policeman, the risk of slipping that small book into the trunk was too great. There might be inspections along the way as we traveled to meet our ship in Antwerp. It was just too dangerous to include anything not on the approved list. Well, with one exception. On the evening before our departure, my mother's sister, Aunt Augusta, asked me to take a walk with her. She led me to the chicken coop, lifted its wooden threshold and uncovered a metal box. From it, she took my mother's engagement ring. Aunt Augusta told me to put the ring into the cuff of my socks and only give to Mutti after we crossed the German border. I agreed. She explained that my parents had shown her this hiding place and offered its contents to her and Uncle Adolph should the need arise. I handled a heavy gold chain and some rings before restoring these items to their hiding place. Whether my relatives ever had the opportunity to empty this little cache, I do not know.

On December 10, Hugo Kliem took us to the train station in his horse-drawn wagon. He wiped his eyes with his red handkerchief. When it was time to say goodbye, he bent down to kiss my mother. She gently pushed him away, pointed to the other passengers at the station said one word: "*Rassenschande.*"[4]

Hugo nodded and, with tears running down into his beard, he climbed back into the wagon and turned his team homeward.

When we crossed from Germany into Holland, I reached into my sock and handed my mother her engagement ring. I think she was glad to have it but Papa was angry; what Aunt Augusta and I had done could have cost us our freedom, perhaps our lives.

In Amsterdam, we had a brief but joyous reunion of two days with Jup, the slimmer, stronger version of our Dicker. We expected he would soon leave for Palestine or join us in America. Walter seemed safe in England. We did not know that in the spring the Netherlands would be occupied by the Nazis and Walter would be imprisoned as an "enemy alien" and sent to Australia.

Meanwhile, my cousin Margot had left Germany via Italy during the *Sitzkrieg* months. Her parents may have been among the last Jews to escape. They traveled in a sealed railroad car across France to Lisbon, Portugal, where they boarded a ship for the United States. The German conquest of its western neighbors began just a few weeks after their escape. The Moses family—my Aunt Anna, Uncle Jakob, and cousins, Ruth and her husband Max, Josef, and Margot, all reunited in Minnesota, a state fortunate to have received such wonderful new citizens. However, we did not learn of the fate of the extended family, the relatives we left behind in Winzig, for decades after the end of the war.

NOTES

1. I was especially troubled about this gap in memory until Margot told me of a similar problem. She is unable to recall her stay in Trieste while waiting for her ship to America. Also, my friend Anita Frank was twelve when he parents placed her on a Kindertransport to England. She remembers waving goodbye as the train pulled out in Berlin, but nothing else until arriving in Scotland.
2. Backshirts were members of the Nazi military.
3. Recall Grynspan was the young man who shot a German embassy secretary, triggering Nazis' use of the incident as a pretense to carry out *Kristallnacht.*
4. *Rassenschande*, the defilement of race, was a serious criminal offence in Nazi Germany. A kiss between Aryan and Jew could be interpreted as such and result in concentration camp as a penalty for both participants.

Chapter 6

From Farm to Farm

Crossing the Atlantic by ship in December is rarely easy; storms are the rule rather than the exception. Our journey from Antwerp, Belgium, to Hoboken, New Jersey, was scheduled to take a week but stretched into ten interminable, stomach-wrenching, head-pounding days and nights. The first delay, however, was not related to the weather; it was due to the negligence of Winzig's Mayor Lang. He would have been pleased to know he detained an ocean liner for several hours in the rough waters of the English Channel.

The *SS Pennland* of the Holland America Line was crowded with refugees fleeing the Nazis. She flew the Dutch flag and thus was subject to search and seizure according to international law. Belligerents, as were England and Germany since September 1939, could board a neutral vessel and examine its manifests and cargo. Passengers' passports were held in a safe in the captain's quarters and could be scrutinized. Should items listed as contraband, for example military equipment, be on board, they could be confiscated. In some cases, the entire ship could be towed into port and the crew held until the end of hostilities. A similar concept applied to individuals deemed potentially or actually dangerous. The officer in charge of the search and seizure operation had the right to determine if any passengers should be removed.

Our cargo consisted of thousands of caged canaries; a more innocent freight is hard to imagine. Nevertheless, the *Pennland* lay anchored in the English Channel for several hours while a small motorboat flying the Union Jack was tied alongside. British naval officers had come aboard to examine the vessel and the search seemed to take an inordinately long time. These were mine-infested waters and some passengers were getting concerned. What was wrong? What can't we get underway?

As for me, I was barely aware of the delay. Earlier, I had noticed a member of the crew throwing dead canaries overboard and had asked where they came from. He explained, and I offered to help with their care. He took me below into a wondrous world of yellow feathers, alive with trilling songs, sweet chirping, and fluttering wings. Thousands of German-bred birds were on their way to America.

"I would love to work with them, would that be possible?" I asked.

Someone went to ask the person in charge, while I tiptoed around this avian delight. I was down there perhaps an hour when a Dutch sailor tapped my shoulder:

"Are you Rita Steinhardt?"

"Yes."

"You are wanted in the captain's cabin. Please follow me."

Bewildered and excited, I followed him up and down several staircases. Finally, he knocked on a door. We entered and, to my amazement, I saw Friedel and my parents seated there. Standing nearby, I recognized the captain of the *Pennland* and two naval officers in English uniforms. Before I could say a word, the older of the Englishmen said: "Yes, I see what you mean. You may sail."

A shaking of hands and then everybody got up and walked out. Mutti and Papa looked relieved and Friedel shook his head. I stood there with my mouth open. I seemed to have walked into the final scene of a play to which I had no script. Not until we were alone was I given an explanation: The English boarding party had inspected the manifest of the ship and reviewed the passports of all passengers. When the officer came across Siegfried Steinhardt, aged 18, with no "J" on the cover of the document, he became suspicious. He wanted to meet that young man, and possibly take him into custody. Why? The English knew that the Germans attached potential undercover agents to families going to the United States. Once in America, these agents crossed the border into Canada and, from there, boarded a ship to England. My brother, a German spy? I thought the notion hilarious, but my parents and Friedel were not amused. They had been through several anxious hours. Their inability to speak English had made it difficult to follow the dialogue, but clearly our captain and the English officers had had a heated argument. The Dutch master of the *Pennland* refused to allow the forced removal of one of his passengers on a vague suspicion; he believed Siegfried to be a legitimate member of the Steinhardt family. It was my mother who broke the deadlock. She did that with just two words: "Find Rita." Find me they did, eventually, among the canaries. One look at me and the British naval officer declared himself satisfied to leave without my brother; the resemblance between brother and sister was undeniable.

Underway again, the stormy weather made most of the passengers and even some members of the crew miserably sea sick. There were moments when I hoped we'd hit a mine that would end this agony. The open deck, despite the damp and penetrating cold, eased my nausea. Occasionally, my brother and I found ourselves hanging onto the same spot on the railing. As we neared the shore of our new homeland, Friedel surprised me by asking how I really felt about being Jewish.

"I'm not sure," I replied. "I know I'm supposed to be proud and chosen by God and all that, but chosen for what?"

"Mostly to suffer," Friedel said, "and I don't want to suffer any more."

"Neither do I. But what can we do about it?"

"I've been thinking about converting to Christianity."

"No! Seriously? Would you really? Such a thing never entered my mind."

"You understand it has nothing to do with religion," Friedel clarified. "I don't have any faith in any God."

I was stunned and probably for the first time realized he was an individual, a young man in his own right, not merely a part of my family. Friedel was the nickname for Siegfried, the hero of Germanic mythology, but in that moment on the deck of the *Pennland*, he began to change into Freddy. We watched the angry sea for a few more minutes and then I told him that I used to pray a lot, but stopped a while ago. But convert? That seemed like joining the enemy. Why?

He said, "I want to fit in."

How neatly Friedel-now-Freddy had expressed my own need to belong, to feel at home in the world, to walk along any street and be a part of the scene, to stop being different because different meant inferior. But, at the same time, I wondered if this desire for acceptance was a flaw, a weakness of character in his nature and in mine as well. I wanted to stop being the *Untermensch* and start to feel equal to others. But were the strong the leaders, not individuals who stood above the crowd? I realized I wanted to be both. I wanted to be part of the herd and also something more than that. How could I aspire to be "a someone," a person with a mind of her own who nevertheless belonged? These bewildering, contradictory emotions rolled through me. After some minutes of silence, I nodded.

"You are right. After we settle in America, we'll do it, we'll become Christians. Mutti won't care, Papa will. But we'll worry about that later."

By now, we were shivering with cold, so we made our way to the dining room for a cup of hot chocolate. It tasted wonderful.

My parents were in their fifties when we boarded the *Pennland*; and, aside from the 40 Marks in our pockets, we had had nothing. But, we had relatives in the New World. My mother's brother Albert had written he would buy a farm for us and we could gradually repay the cost. Albert had emigrated when he was eighteen, settled in New York, and married into a well-off family. He and his wife had no children. Over the years, his import/export business flourished and Albert became a wealthy man. Unlike most of the passengers on the *Pennland*, we were fortunate to be spared the uncertainties facing most newcomers. Our future seemed assured. Surely, just like German soil, American fields needed plowing, seeding, and harvesting; American cows gave milk from comparable udders; and American horses worked as hard as those across the sea. We would manage. Freddy expected to help Papa with light chores until he found his own way and I, now sixteen years old, was eager to get back to school.

We knew so little.

After reading every Karl May paperback, my brother and I expected to meet Indians with plumed headdresses on the sidewalks of New York. The little I thought I knew about American history was gleaned from my repeated reading of *Vom Winde Verweht*, the German translation of Margaret Mitchell's *Gone with the Wind*. But I had misunderstood the meaning of North vs. South. I thought the war involved the continents, South America and North America. In our defense, we had no access to the truth. Anti-American Nazi propaganda was so implausible it bordered on the ridiculous. The newspapers referred to US President Franklin Delano Roosevelt as the Jew Rosenfeld. Photographs of slums and exaggerated crime statistics painted the United States to be a country in lawless chaos, dominated by Jews, gangsters, and other unsavory characters. We had no concept of the diversity of the nation, its democratic institutions, or the vastness of its geography. A display of my ignorance began on day of our arrival.

Uncle Albert and Aunt Flo, in their pristine car, met us in Hoboken, New Jersey, where the *Pennland* had docked. We had not sighted the Statue of Liberty as we sailed into port, so during the ride to Brooklyn,

I sat with my forehead pressed against the car window, avid for my first glimpses of America. The appearance of a man walking along the sidewalk caused me to call out to my aunt:

"I just saw a chimney sweep."

"Did you? How odd."

"Yes. And there is one more."

"Are you sure? If you spot another, call me quickly."

"There! There! There is one standing on the corner."

Auntie followed my pointing finger, then smiled and said, "He is not a chimney sweep. He is a Negro."

The only black faces I had ever seen belonged to the men who were covered with soot because they cleaned flues and smokestacks. "I have so much to learn," I thought.

During our first three months in this country, while Uncle Albert and my father searched for a farm, the family was split up among various relatives. My temporary home was in the Bronx at Papa's oldest sister, Aunt Rebecka. She was a widow, tall, a little stooped, with strong features. She had reared her five children single-handedly. Her deceased husband, according to family gossip, had been handsome, charming, and fond of expensive suits. Unfortunately, he spent his time at the racetrack while Rebecka took care of their candy store. I was told that when her children were infants, she kept them in shoeboxes on the store's counter and nursed them behind a curtain in the shop. Her three sons and two daughters were adults when I came into the picture, but only the youngest girl had married and left home.

On my first morning in the Bronx, when I sat down for breakfast, I was surprised and pleased to see an entire box of corn flakes on the table. Recognizing the box from my *Haustochter* stint in Berlin when the flakes were kept under lock and key, I asked my aunt how many pieces I could have. The question seemed to puzzle her. She shrugged her shoulders and exchanged my bowl with a larger one. This she filled and pointed to the milk and sugar. What wonderful, crunchy spoonfuls! "Ah, beautiful America," I thought.

During the three months of my stay in the Bronx, I never quite figured out who slept where in the cramped apartment. My spot was the living room couch. There was a certain grimness about Aunt Rebecka. She was quick to take offense when none was intended, and I never her saw her display any tenderness. But, she was good of heart. The poorest of our relatives, she was always first to offer help to the immigrants from Europe. When Ruth and Max first arrived, she gave them a roof over their heads until HIAS loaned them bus fare to Minneapolis. Decades later, Ruth and I were still trying to figure out if or how Aunt Rebecka's sons earned a living. They certainly kept unusual hours.

My cousin Joanna, the married daughter, was a teacher and thus the logical one to take me to register at Richmond Hill High School. We rode the subway, a breathtaking first for a girl from Winzig. I was accepted into the ninth grade and was given a schedule and some textbooks. Joanna tried to explain how to pay for a ride on the underground, how many stations I needed to pass to get to school, on which staircase to exit, where to turn right, and how far to walk until I saw the school. It was a lot to take in. My English was minimal and my pronunciation beyond the grasp of nearly everyone; at best I was on par with an American three-year-old.

By sheer chance, I got through my first day without mishaps. After that, it was touch and go. If Cousin Jo mentioned that more than one line of trains came into the subway station nearest to the apartment, I missed that part. So, every morning I just boarded the first train that came along. Sometimes I reached my destination on the first attempt and sometimes I did not. My trips were not quite as haphazard after I noticed that to reach the school the name of the first stop must begin with the letter "A." If it did not, I needed to get off the train, cross the platform, return to my starting point, and try again. Eventually, I realized that only the train marked with a "G" went in the correct direction.

This wonderful discovery ended my wandering in the wilderness of New York's underground. Why no one asked me why I was so often late to school, I cannot say. Or perhaps they did, but I did not understand. On a really bad day, the fifteen-minute trip could take over an hour.

I never told anyone about my transportation misadventures and I was too intimidated by this new world to ask anyone to for assistance. Nor did I explain my language difficulty to the teacher of the music class of perhaps seventy or eighty students. He called on me during my first week and I did not understand his question. The kindhearted girl sitting next to me whispered, "Tell him you're new in the country." But that I could not do. The very thought of revealing myself as an outsider was mortifying. The need to be just like everyone else was stronger than my shame at standing dumbstruck before my classmates and the instructor. Years later, I understood this overpowering urge for acceptance; having been branded an *Untermensch*, it would take time for that stain to fade and eventually disappear.

Despite my loneliness in the midst of so many people, I was not unhappy during my stay in the Bronx. I was living with relatives I did not know who surely were not delighted to feed an extra mouth and cede their sofa to me. So, I willingly helped with the chores, made no complaints about my aunt's tasteless meals, and spent my free time studying, even after my aunt grumbled that my late nights raised her electric bill. Fun and games were not on the horizon, although I remember an outing with Hilda, Aunt Rebecka's older daughter. She loved ice hockey, and one Sunday she took me to a game at Madison Square Garden. I had no idea what I was watching; I enjoyed the exciting atmosphere, but would not look at the violence on the rink below. Away from my family and too insecure to make friends, I was content to observe life, not live it, to read and learn, as I reduced my German/English dictionary to tatters. My first report card was encouraging, all Cs and Bs except an F in Music.

Uncle Albert and my father found a suitable farm in April. It was located a few miles from Pine Bush in the beautiful foothills of New

York's Orange County. The owner of the property wanted simply to walk away from everything, taking nothing but personal belongings with him. But, Uncle Albert had changed his mind. He no longer wanted to buy the property for my father. He bought it for himself—as a tax shelter. My parents and brother were to be his indentured servants. This was a shocking disappointment. For the moment, we could do nothing but accept this arrangement. The land, some three hundred acres, came with a herd of more than thirty cows, two horses, pigs, poultry, barns, farm equipment, and a handsome, two-story house. Along with the machinery and the animals, we also inherited John, a Polish immigrant who had worked there for years.

My mother was ill and unable to join us for our first two weeks on the farm. Thus, I was thrust into the role of the homemaker. The large, white farmhouse at the end of a long driveway resembled a picture postcard scene, but the pleasing image masked incredibly filthy conditions within. The former occupants had thrown their garbage down the steps leading from the kitchen into the basement. Only after Papa removed seven wagonloads of rubbish did we discover a cement floor. Clearing out the cellar disturbed the rats. They came upstairs, big, ugly, some with moss on their backs. John used a heavy shovel while I stood on a chair and peeked through my fingers as he killed them one by one. Every surface in the kitchen was caked with grime, every pot and pan had to be scrubbed before it could be used. I tried, but it was my mother who gradually, over many weeks, turned this sty into a spotless home.

My skill to prepare decent meals left much to be desired, but the victims of my dinners were too kind to complain. When I placed a package of raw bacon on John's plate, he ate it, suggesting that in future I might fry the slices. Yet, to share meals with him required fortitude. Upon sitting down at the table, he would quite casually remove his upper and lower dental plates and put them into the front pocket of his overalls. When the dessert and coffee were served, he would reach for the teeth, blow off the bits of straw that now adhered to them, and snap them back into his mouth. We tried not to notice, but one day my brother and I lost all composure. John sneezed and his dentures flew across the kitchen table, skittered across the floor, and came to rest under the stove. Freddy and I laughed until we gasped for air. We were sorry to hurt John's feelings, though. He was a good man, a hard worker, and every month he asked me to write a note to his son and enclose some money in the envelope. I never met the boy, but I was shown his picture many times. How John had managed to get into this country, I never knew. He was illiterate, unable even to sign his name. He never went to town and he avoided all contact with strangers. On the several occasions when the Immigration Department sent an agent to check if we were actually farming, John seemed very nervous and stayed in his room.

When the house was in respectable shape, Uncle Albert and Aunt Flo visited frequently. My Mutti was a fine cook, and they enjoyed her meals. But my aunt was a city woman; she found country life boring. Soon, Albert came alone. He scrutinized the records of the milk sold daily to the creamery; monitored the bills for seed, fertilizer, and other necessities; and complained how expensive it was to maintain the farm. His secretary kept the accounts; we never knew if the farm was self-supporting, making; or losing money. My parents received no salary, only reimbursement of approved expenses. My mother was distressed to have to ask her brother for five dollars if she needed to buy a pair of shoes. I had no money, but I really did not need any. Aunt Flo's cast-off clothing was nicer than anything I had ever owned before and, most importantly, these discards made me look like an American girl.

Freddy and I were, however, troubled by this demeaning state of affairs. When we discussed it with Papa, he reminded us that his brother-in-law helped to save us from Hitler. Papa would not upset that relationship. Freddy and I were in no position to suggest any alternatives, so we had to bide our time. I had started school the day my mother recovered from her illness and joined us on the farm, but Freddy was at loose ends during our first year in America. He was not able to do the hard labor of a farm hand. Yes, he was proud of his driver's license, ran errands to town, and took care of the red tape that inevitably pursued us. But that was not enough. When, on December 7, 1941, the United States entered the Second World War, Freddy tried again and again to join a branch of the Armed Forces. He went to three different recruiting stations, but was rejected the moment a doctor placed a stethoscope on his chest.

Meanwhile, my dislike of Uncle Albert had become revulsion. He had come for the weekend, again without his wife. His room was next to mine and one night I felt hands groping my body. A familiar voice murmured, "I just want you to be nice to me." Pretending to be asleep, I moved myself into the fetal position and said "*Pfui*," a German exclamation of disgust that defies translation. Uncle Albert sighed and left the room. My heart was hammering against my chest as I lay awake. What should I do? If I told my father, he would beat up his brother-in-law and might land in jail. If I told my mother, she would be devastated. I decided to swear Freddy to secrecy and seek his advice. Meanwhile, I dreaded seeing our supposed benefactor at breakfast the next morning. I need not have worried. He was way ahead of me. Coming down the staircase, I heard Uncle Albert tell my mother that she must remind me to shut off the light when I went to bed, that he had to go into my room during the night and turn it off.

Freddy listened to my account with hands balled into fists. He showed me how to place a chair against the doorknob and, after some consideration, he proposed a scheme that would punish our uncle and benefit all of us: blackmail the bastard.

"Have you lost your mind?" I asked.

"Not at all," Freddy replied. "This is my plan. You leave your bedroom door open. He'll take that as an invitation. I'll be in the closet with a camera. When he comes near you, I snap a picture and we've got him. What do you say?"

"I won't do any such thing. Forget it."

"Why not? We could force him into a new arrangement for Mutti and Papa."

"I just couldn't. So let it go."

Rather reluctantly, Freddy dropped his extortion scheme. I barricaded my door every night, but Uncle Albert never bothered me again. He found a willing partner down the road, a frequent visitor at a neighbor's house. The lady, a divorcee with two children, manipulated him quite skillfully. First, she became his mistress. Then, she threatened to end their fun unless he divorced his wife and marry her. Within a couple of years, the new Mrs. Moses had isolated her husband from every member of his family.

Yet, the emancipation of my parents from their emotional and financial bondage was initiated halfway across the world, in Australia. Yes, it was Walter who provided the spur. He and I had maintained our own correspondence ever since he left home. I had kept him apprised of the one-sided arrangement foisted on our parents. After two years of work with nothing to show for it, Papa's gratitude was wearing thin. Under the right circumstances, he and my mother might be willing to strike out on their own. Such right circumstances resulted from Walter's friendship with Rudy, a fellow detainee at Camp Hay.

Rudy's sister lived New York City. Her close friends were Katrin Holland and her husband, also émigrés from Nazi Germany. They had done well in the United States; he traded on Wall Street, she was successful writer of spy and mystery novels. They owned a house and eighty acres in Pattenburg, New Jersey, amid rolling hills near the Pennsylvania border. They had renovated the house, which they used as a weekend and summer retreat. The problem was maintaining it. The Hollands had been unable to find the help to make their stays comfortable. Both were useless in the kitchen and they had failed to find a person or couple to work as caretaker, gardener, and cook. Walter suggested I make further inquiries.

I said nothing to my parents or Freddy because nothing might came of this pie in the sky, but I decided to pursue the possibilities. My first step was to telephone Katrin at the Royalton Hotel, where the Hollands resided. She listened with increasing interest as I explained the purpose of my call. After a brief conversation with her husband, Katrin asked if I would come to New York to meet with them. I was ecstatic and barely kept my composure when I assured her that I would come.

My hands were clammy when I walked from Grand Central Station to the hotel a few weeks later. The couple greeted me warmly, had tea and cookies waiting, and quickly relieved much of my nervousness. We spoke for about an hour. I answered many questions and then it was time to leave to catch my train. The needle had been threaded, whether or not the stitches would hold was out of my hands. Katrin said she planned to call my parents and arrange to a meeting. I left the hotel with a mixture of elation and anxiety. Was I meddling? In over my head? Would Mutti and Papa think I, their youngest, had overstepped her place?

I need not have worried. Within a few months, Mutti and Papa lived in Pattenburg, New Jersey. They had made the move. Freddy had helped with the arrangements. Even Rexy, a Shepherd-Collie mix acquired in Pine Bush, adjusted quickly. Papa leased the land and both my parents were paid for work not connected to the running of the farm. The Hollands had their own quarters, and my parents lived in the rest of the house. Mutti cooked for them and their occasional guests. Papa began to turn the fallow acres into a viable farm and planted flowers and fruit trees.

In winter, my parents might have been lonely. If they were, they never complained. Mutti read and knitted and enjoyed her music on the radio. Papa looked after the animals and prepared the bulbs that would bloom gloriously in the spring. Both were avid in keeping track of the war in Europe; a wall map pinpointed the positions of the Allied and Axis armies. They subscribed to the German-Jewish newspaper *Der Aufbau*, which carried stories about the atrocities committed by the Nazis. Paramount in their thoughts was Jup. Could he survive the brutal German occupation of the Netherlands? News from him would lift a great burden from their otherwise contented life in Pattenburg. In this anxiety, they were not alone; it was shared by millions of parents whose sons were battling the Nazis on three continents.

Chapter 7

'If She Wants to Do This, She Will'

It is difficult not to become emotional, even a little teary-eyed, as I recall my good fortune to attend Pine Bush Central High School in Orange County, New York. The kindness and guidance shown me, a new arrival from another world, made it possible for me to graduate with a New York Regents diploma in two years. The principal allowed me to combine ninth and tenth grade classes during my first year, and eleventh and twelfth grades in the next. He arranged for me to take the most advanced German Regents examination in Newburgh, the nearest town to offer it. This allowed me to me to receive my diploma at eighteen, at the same age as most other students.

There were fewer than twenty students at my graduation ceremony; I do not recall the sale of a class ring or a yearbook, in any case, I wouldn't have been able to afford either one. Our prom cost nothing, it was held in a large barn; refreshments were donated and served by the PTA. The music teacher provided a band to play dance music, and everyone went home soon after midnight. Such simplicity wasn't considered paucity; we enjoyed ourselves without bankrupting the family. Frugality was the community lifestyle, whether due to necessity or by choice I cannot say. The school had been built to instruct, nothing more. We had no gymnasium, no swimming pool, no marching band, no sports teams. During recess, we played baseball in the yard or did some calisthenics. But, when it came to the faculty, Pine Bush excelled. The dozen or so teachers brought their personal warmth and relaxed approach into the classroom. Learning, rather than grades, was the focus. Lacking a guidance staff, those of us who needed help went to any of our teachers for support.

Each morning, I hurried to meet the school bus at the end of the driveway and eagerly climbed aboard. As we went from farm to farm, the seats filled and the atmosphere grew noisy with conversation and laughter. Within a few weeks, I felt welcome among these American teenagers who greeted me with friendly smiles. I did not become part of a particular circle of friends, nor did I have such unrealistic expectations. These boys and girls had known each other since kindergarten. It would have been difficult to include any newcomer, particularly one who spoke such faltering English. I did make one friend, a lovely girl named Robin who had moved to Pine Bush recently. Both our mothers were welcoming when we stayed at each other's houses overnight. But Robin was seriously searching for *the* boy, an interest I did not share at that time.

Pine Bush Central did not throw me into the American melting pot; the proper symbol for my integration is the salad bowl: each ingredient remains intact but the blend forms a harmonious whole. A foreign arrival can maintain facets from the "old country" and become a proud citizen of the new.

My years in a Prussian classroom had taught me patriotism required obedience to the state, the alternative is chaos. This concept was further broadened, indeed, distorted, by the Nazis, who demanded uniformity of thought and action. The Fuehrer personified the nation, he was the arbiter of right and wrong, his decrees were irrefutable, and questioning his wisdom was not only disloyal, it was criminal. The official ideology left no room for individual judgments. The good citizen was expected to accept and obey: This is the correct shape of the Aryan nose; this is the proper angle of your arm when you give the Hitler salute; race is destiny; war determines the survival of the fittest; this is art, all else is kitsch; this is truth, the only truth. But, at Pine Bush, the give and take, the encouragement to question, to dispute, even to challenge the teachers chipped away at my indoctrination. At that small, rural high school, I learned diversity is constructive and nonconformity is not equivalent to defectiveness. Indeed, in America, to describe something or someone as unique is a compliment. What a liberating idea!

After the attack on Pearl Harbor in December of 1941, I was occasionally asked questions by fellow students about Nazi Germany. Perhaps this was my launch pad for more than fifty years in front of classrooms. There was just one other Jewish student in some of my courses, a boy, but we did not use our shared religion as a basis for friendliness. My parents did not attend any religious services. Both had been raised in Orthodox Jewish families, but now they were content to light the candles on Friday nights, read from the appropriate prayer book on holy days, fast on the Day of Atonement, and keep the dietary laws of Passover. For their four children, being Jewish had become a legacy, not the center of who we were.

I had never heard of St. Valentine and my first acquaintance with this benefactor of single maidens was bittersweet. I understood greeting cards would be exchanged during homeroom and I was certain that I would receive none. I had not yet met Robin nor made any close friends. How mortifying if I were the only one left empty-handed. I asked my mother for a dime and bought a card at the drugstore near the school. The wording was pretty innocuous. I addressed it to myself, signed it "Guess Who?" and placed into the heart-shaped box in the classroom. Delighted as well as chagrinned, I found two more greetings addressed to me and I was the subject of quite a bit of teasing as to who my secret "Guess Who" admirer might be.

I had so much to learn! I studied lipstick and nail polish, saddle shoes and hairstyles, popular songs, and American football. For the first time, I tasted ice cream sodas, hamburgers with ketchup, a fresh pineapple, and the strange tang of Coca-Cola. In Germany, most holidays were religious or political, generally observed with solemnity. American celebrations were more joyful. The achievements of the past, whether by Columbus, St. Patrick, or the founders of the nation were occasions for picnics, parades, and fireworks.

My teachers, doubling as advisors, encouraged me to go to college. Was it possible? We had no money. Indeed, when I told the family what I hoped to do, my not-yet-blackmailed-away Uncle Albert butted in:

"Who do you think you are? You're nothing but a little refugee girl. Don't expect any help from me."

Those words stung. I was ready to give a flippant answer when my father answered for me:

"We don't want anything from you. If she wants to do this, she will."

One of the teachers told me about scholarships and she helped me secure and fill out the required forms for admittance to several universities. One, a religious institution in Tennessee, offered complete package: room, board, and tuition. But my advisor shook his head: "Not for you. They will try to convert you."

To be honest, my choice to apply to the University of South Carolina was a direct result of my crush on the biology teacher. USC was his alma mater. The day after the Tennessee school tempted me, I received, and, with the approval of my mentors, accepted, a USC scholarship. I would be given the opportunity to work in the library, which would cover the cost of the room; I could help in the dining hall and receive free meals. The cost of tuition for out of state students was one hundred dollars per semester, no matter how many classes one took. My family was pleased, even proud, and I was elated.

That summer, I needed to make money. The farm was in the foothills of the Catskill Mountains, an area dubbed the Borsht Belt. In the 1940s, this region was dominated by dozens of hotels, the favorite summer destination of Jewish clientele from New York City. Surely, I could make beds, scrub vegetables, help in the kitchen, clean rooms, weed lawns, whatever. Freddy offered to drive me from hotel to hotel until I found a job. On our second stop, Shawanga Lodge, I was hired. Just like that. The salary was more than I expected, the work less challenging than I imagined. What luck! I was employed to take care of the hotel owners' one-year-old baby. Later, I learned I had appeared at a moment of desperate need; both parents worked long hours in the running of the hotel and they hoped I could fill in until they found a proper nanny. I stayed the entire summer, slept in a lovely room with Baby Alan, and my excellent meals were delivered to our shared room.

Within a few days, I mastered the routine of feeding, bathing, rocking, and diapering my charge and we grew attached to each other. Several times a day, his parents looked in on us for a few minutes, and Mondays I was free to do as I pleased. I liked my work, but sometimes I was lonely for some company closer to my age. After all, the place was swarming with college students. They waited on tables, manicured lawns, instructed all sports activities, played in the band, took care of guests' children, and more. Most were young men, though there were a few young women as well. The work was hard, but one summer in the borscht belt could pay tuition for two semesters. I once glimpsed their sleeping quarters and knew their mothers would have been horrified.

The wages paid by the hotel management were small part of the staff's income, their major earnings came from tips. Woe to the family that was miserly in handing out gratuities; they waited longest for their meals, were handed soup with a thumb resting in it, found tennis courts already occupied, and the best seats at shows previously reserved. After a few days, the relationship between good tipping and good service became clear and the numbers on the bills handed out grew bigger.

On the days when Alan's mother took care of him, I explored the grounds and enjoyed conversations with some of the college students.

I had so many questions concerning college life, and found everyone informative and friendly. My accent raised some polite inquiries, and I was willing to share some of my personal experiences in Nazi Germany. Nearly all the young men expected to be in the Armed Forces before long.

Every evening, the band played dance music in one of the pavilions. At first I was content to listen on the steps outside. Then, I began to watch through the open door. What fun! Ladies in their colorful, summer frocks whirled about on the arms of their well-muscled partners. After a closer look, I wondered if I had blundered onto a mother-son dance party; the women seemed rather mature, their companions much younger. I walked in and sat down on one of the chairs. I did not remain on the sidelines long, a handsome, tanned young man asked me to join the couples on the floor. I was thrilled. He asked:

"Well, well, what are you doing here? What's your name and what room are you in?"

"My name is Rita, and I take care of the owners' child. My room is in the main house, next to theirs."

"Ah-ha, so you're part of the hired help. I thought you were too good to be true. We'd better stop dancing before we get into trouble."

"What trouble? I'm new at this, please, explain."

"My name is Marty and I think you're cute and I'll be a perfect gentleman and put you into the picture. Let's walk outside. I don't want the powers-that-be to see us together."

During the next ten minutes, Marty gave me the short course on Catskills protocol. At first I did not believe him, but later conversations confirmed his every word. My mother had been right when she warned me to be careful, to remember *"Oben hui, unten pfui,"* a rather earthy, German version of "all that glitters is not gold."

Marty explained: "I'm one of the swimming instructors. It's a good job, practically pays my college tuition. But my contract has some hidden clauses. All the fellows here have the same agreement. Nothing is written down, you understand, but it's part of the job. I'm expected to entertain some of the single ladies when I'm not working at the pool. Some of them get bored with just female company and that could be bad for business. The dance allows us and the ladies a chance to decide how far our acquaintance will take us."

"So you have to dance with them?"

"Exactly, and perform any other services they might require."

"Do you mean what I think you mean?"

He shrugged his shoulders. I understood.

"I saw wedding bands. Where are the husbands?"

"They work in the city and come on weekends."

"Do they know?"

Marty gave me a sidelong smile. I tried to appear sophisticated, but actually I was shocked. Neither Marty nor I wanted to jeopardize our paychecks, so we said good night and returned to our chores, he to his lonely ladies, I to baby Alan. Repelled and fascinated, I wanted to learn more. Every day as I pushed the baby carriage around the grounds, I managed to exchange a "Hello. What's up?" with some staff member and thus continued my education on Borscht Belt culture.

My favorite lecturer on this topic was Josh, who told a modern version of the *Canterbury Tales*. One night, he was entertaining his favorite grass-widow (the name for a woman who only had weekend visits from her husband) in her room when her husband made an unexpected appearance. As the cuckold put his key in the door, Josh jumped from the bed, grabbed his clothes, and jumped, buck naked, out the window. He landed in some bushes and wanted to show me the full extent of his injuries. As soon as I managed to stop laughing, I politely declined the offer.

Although I made no close friend among the staff members, I was able to gain some insights beyond the fun and games: their concerns about parents, money, the international problems facing the country. Should a young man enlist or wait to be drafted? Which branch of the Armed Forces would be his best option? They knew the war in Europe and in the Pacific would be their war, that the world outside Shawanga Lodge was about to claim them. Although they would have scoffed at the acclaim, they were about to become part of the Greatest Generation.

As for me, when I left the lodge I used a large part of my summer wages to pay for a train ticket to Columbia, South Carolina. With the rest, I bought a suitcase, a pair of vaunted saddle shoes, and skirts and blouses—my first new clothes in many years. This was August of 1942 and as I packed to start life as a co-ed, these purchases gave me a new confidence. In my new wallet, I had a check with Papa's signature for one hundred dollars, tuition for my first semester, and enough money to keep me eating for the first several days. I planned to study journalism. The power of words had attracted me since I learned to read. History was a natural adjunct, an outgrowth of the Nazi years, of the war, and of my concern over the fate of my brother Jup. The university admissions officer had assured me I would be able to earn enough to cover any additional expenses while attending classes. So, my head filled with excitement and optimism, and my heart bursting with gratitude for the possibilities America offered this refugee from Winzig, I stepped from New York's Grand Central Station onto the southbound train.

CHAPTER 8

TELLING FORTUNES

The USC campus in the capital of city of Columbia was beautiful, worthy of a picture postcard. Brick paths connected ivy-covered buildings, statues of Southern heroes watched over jade green lawns, students greeted those they did and did not know with a "hi" and a "how are ya?" My roommate was Terry from New York, and we shared a bathroom with two girls next door. We kept our place neat. Terry had brought matching bedspreads and curtains, our books were lined up on shelves above our desks; and we never received a reprimand after surprise room inspections. Floors and bathrooms were washed once a week by an elderly black maid. All dormitories were supervised by a housemother. Ours, Mrs. Sims, was a Southern lady who wore gloves when she went out. She presided in the lobby. We signed her ledger whenever we left the building in the evening and later recorded the time of our return. Gentlemen callers had to be properly introduced to her, and she knew the genealogy of most of the Southern students. We had no keys. The outer doors were locked at 10 pm during the week and twelve on Saturday nights. If you were tardy, you had to knock on Mrs. Sims' window. A moment later, she would emerge in her fuzzy robe and hairnet and greet you with a lecture on the behavior of proper young women.

As soon as I registered for my courses, I hurried to the Student Aid Office and asked about work on campus. Because I was eligible for a Federal Youth Administration scholarship, I was assigned to my favorite place, the grand library. The pay was twenty-five cents per hour, and the work at the check-out desk was easy. I still needed to provide for my meals, so I introduced myself to the director of Food Services, who welcomed me into her kitchen. In return for helping to serve food at the steam table twice a day, I was welcome to three meals. The choice of what I ate was entirely mine. It was almost too good to be true. If I had a better voice, I might have sung "America, the Beautiful" after that interview. What a country! I could study, eat well, and sleep in comfort.

I kept both campus jobs until my graduation three-and-a-half years later. For pocket money, I needed some further employment. Most fortunate was my introduction to Professor Frank Wardlaw. He taught all the journalism classes and became my mentor. A tall, fine-looking Southern gentleman whose lung condition exempted him from service in the Armed Forces, he wore many hats related to campus affairs. He treated me without condensation, was always available, and encouraged my hopes. As director of the Alumni Office, he hired me to run the mimeograph machine, stuff envelopes, and do whatever else needed to be done. During my sophomore year, Professor Wardlaw's connection to South Carolina's major newspaper, the *Columbia Record*, led to my first journalism paycheck; I wrote a monthly column on life in Nazi Germany. When he and his wife asked if I could baby-sit their infant son on an occasional Saturday night, I felt honored, but lost the argument not to accept payment. His solicitude for me was also instrumental in arranging my first speaking engagement. Soon, I was asked to present talks about Nazi Germany all over the state. Word spread, as the Elks told the PTA, who notified the DAR, who passed my name to a garden club, and so on. Occasionally, participants from the audience engaged in angry disagreements on US policy and asked me, all 110 pounds and five feet of me, to settle the dispute. I traveled on buses, occasionally accepted rides, and once or twice hitchhiked to my next commitment.

My listeners were appreciative, rewarded me with pen and pencil sets, and sometimes a small check. The payment was not important, but the boost to my self-confidence was. That was certainly true when Governor Olin Johnson attended one of my speeches and officially declared me an honorary South Carolinian. My undergraduate years resulted in another valued gift: my accent was softened by the gentle tones of Southern speech. No longer was I automatically asked, "So, where are you from?"

I liked nearly all my classes at USC, and did well in writing and in history. I avoided mathematics courses, a regrettable and regretted gap in my education. But, I still had much to learn of things not found in textbooks. For example, during my first two or three weeks at the university, I was delighted to accept invitations to several afternoon teas. I attended as many as time permitted, happy to meet so many friendly young women who seemed interested in me and provided tasty little sandwiches and dainty cupcakes. When these requests for my presence stopped as the demands of classes intensified, I barely noticed. Shortly thereafter, I received another sort of summons. Beautiful Evelyn, a student a few years older than most, asked if she could speak with me in private. I was flattered as well as curious. Evelyn was married and had returned to complete her degree when her officer husband was sent overseas. We met in a corner of the library and the usually unflappable Evelyn seemed ill at ease. She began:

"Rita, I'm so sorry to be the bearer of bad news."

"What? Why? Have I done something wrong?"

"No, no, you're fine. All the girls like you. But, you can't join our sorority because you're on a scholarship. That's against the rules. Don't think you were blackballed; there wasn't a single vote against you. It's just that we can't make exceptions. I hope you understand—and I'm so sorry."

I was completely baffled. What was she talking about? I said nothing, trying to grasp the meaning of her words. My silence seemed to upset

Evelyn further, and she took my hand as if to comfort me as I shook my head in confusion. Finally I asked:

"What is this black ball? And what do you mean, 'sorority'? It's a word I don't know."

Now it was Evelyn's turn to look bewildered. It never occurred to her that I didn't know what "rushing" was, that I had no idea I was being evaluated for sorority membership while munching tiny sandwiches. She sputtered a bit, but I was able to follow her explanation. When she finished, I burst out laughing and then she joined in. In time, she became my best friend and we spent many vacations together at her parents' home.

My first date was pretty much a disaster as well. A young man in one of my classes had the most beautifully sculpted muscles, and he saw my appreciative glances. He asked me on a date and I said fine. When I mentioned his name to one of my dorm mates, she shook her head.

"Are you sure you want to go with him? He's the captain of the football team."

"So, what?" I thought. "She's probably jealous."

Actually, she was trying to warn me that the sports heroes on campus believed girls existed merely or mainly for their entertainment. He picked me up at the dorm in a car, which was pretty unusual, as restrictions on gasoline were already stringent. To my surprise, a freshman member of the team sat behind the steering wheel. My date invited me to join him in the back seat. I sat down, not aware that by accepting, he thought I had no objection to his intentions. The wrestling began almost immediately. We didn't go to eat, or to a movie, or for a walk downtown. We wrestled. He was strong, but I was quick. On the seats, on the floor, we wrestled. Eventually, he realized I was serious about preserving my virginity and, thankfully, rape was not on his agenda. He told me he could have any girl he wanted, so something must be wrong with me to fight like that. I readily agreed to his analysis. In an hour, I was back in the dorm, totally exhausted, and I went to sleep without taking my clothes off. Lesson learned.

The football hero's claim that he could have any girl he wanted was pretty well matched by the availability of dates for every girl in the dorm. This was due to another Columbia, South Carolina, institution: Fort Jackson. During the war, this base, like military installations throughout the country, faced serious challenges of sudden growth. Many thousands of men were trained there. After all, in 1942 and 1943, the Japanese proved much stronger than anticipated. The fate of Allied armies in Africa was in doubt; the invasion of Nazi Europe was barely in the planning stages. So, new recruits, many of them volunteers, arrived daily at the fort. Its facilities were consistently overcrowded despite continuous expansion. The work to turn civilians into soldiers was formidable. Most of the men standing before their drill sergeants for the first time had never held a weapon. They had been reared in cities, their adjustment from job or school to military life required crossing a physical and mental void. Many universities, including the USC campus in Columbia, became adjuncts to military training. ROTC cadres marched from class to class, preparing young men to become officers.

The residents of Columbia spared no effort to make the city hospitable to the enormous influx of servicemen. Churches synagogues, civic organizations—all extended their welcome. On holidays, soldiers were invited to share family meals. Many bars, restaurants, and amusement parks would not take their money. The United Service Organization was the center of relaxation for the soldiers. Housed in a large and well-equipped building, the USO offered a soundproof music room complete with a variety of classical and popular records, a quiet reading room, nightly movies, frequent live shows, and limitless snacks and non-alcoholic drinks. The biggest draw was the Saturday night dances. Though well-chaperoned, they allowed soldiers to meet girls. Female students at the university were urged to support the troops by our attendance. I don't know what the ratio of males to females was, but my guess is a hundred to one. In other words, there were no lonely girls at the University of South Carolina,

The city wore international dress during the war years. Its streets and shops were enlivened by foreign uniforms and unfamiliar languages. Fort Jackson trained young men who had escaped from Nazi-occupied nations, among them Poles, Frenchmen, Hollanders, Norwegians, Greeks, and others. Many of these men had no news of the fate of their families and wanted nothing as desperately as participation in the liberation of their fatherlands. Among them was Pierre. We met at the USO and arranged a dinner date. He was the proverbially charming Frenchman, but concern for his parents and siblings clouded his enjoyment of the good food served at the Ship Ahoy. I am pleased to claim he probably laughed more during the hour we spent together than he had in months. It's not that I was such an amusing companion, things just happened. It started because I have olive skin and, at the time, my hair was coal black and long. I often braided it, tying the ends with red ribbons. Pierre and I were exchanging memories of our European childhoods when I noticed another diner across the room was staring at me.

"*Mon ami*," I said, "There is a lady watching me. Do I have lipstick on my nose? Lettuce on my teeth?"

"*Non, non, cherie*," he replied and we continued our conversation. But to my surprise, the woman rose from her seat and walked to our table.

"A thousand apologies," she addressed me, "I am sorry to intrude. But I have been troubled by something for such a long time, I feel I must take this opportunity to ask you a question. Do you mind?"

"I don't know that until I hear the question."

"That certainly is fair. I have studied the history of your people and I want you to know how sorry I am for the harm we have done you."

She spoke with a broad Southern accent, nothing remotely German or Jewish about her, and I was nonplussed.

"Could you explain?" I asked, trying to soften the remnants of my German accent.

"It's obvious to me—I hope you don't mind—that you are of pure [American] Indian descent. What we white people have done to you is shameful, just shameful. Not that I would judge or blame you, but would you please tell me if you and the members of your tribe still hate us?"

Pierre was beginning to have a coughing fit into his napkin. I kicked his leg under the table. I might have told her I was about as far from an American Indian as a person could be, but the concern in her face spoke to her earnestness. Was forgiveness mine to give? No, certainly not. But we were at war, and I felt righteous about bringing peace to a troubled soul.

"Madam," I replied as seriously as I could manage, "as far as my people are concerned, the battle axes have been buried."

Reading those Karl May books finally paid off, but Pierre was in danger of choking from concealed laughter. I kicked him again.

"You don't know how happy I am to hear that," my new acquaintance said and she smiled broadly. "Just one more question and I won't intrude any longer. Could you just tell what tribe you are from?"

Uh-oh. I couldn't think of a one. But, just that morning I had learned a new and fascinating word when I asked the name of the substance that covered the floors in so many buildings. Worth a try....

"We are not famous, you understand, not many braves or squaws. We are called the Chattahoochees."

"Ah-ha," she said, "I haven't heard of them, but I'll check at the library."

When she closed the door behind her, my French friend and his German date exploded with laughter. My lie was absurd, but at least one American would sleep easier tonight.

The Chattahoochee incident gave me the perfect opportunity to regale Pierre with a story making the rounds in the city. I cannot vouch to its veracity, but it well may have been true. Fort Jackson also maintained a prisoner of-war camp for German soldiers; most had served in the Afrika Korps. The prisoners were permitted to work in a nearby forest, if they chose to do so. They wore jumpsuits stamped with the letters "POW" on the back and were guarded rather casually. One of the men decided to see a little more of this *Amerika*. One morning, he wore his Afrika Korps uniform, with an open-necked shirt and short pants under his overalls. In the forest, he discarded the POW outfit and made for the highway. With his thumb in the air, he had no trouble getting a ride. He knew no English and had no idea he was sitting in the car of the local sheriff who took him for "one of them foreigners." They drove all the way to the famed Myrtle Beach amusement park. There; the sheriff gave the POW some money, and wished him well. What a great place this was, a carousel, many rides, all that that food, even music! The German knew he'd be caught sooner or later, but this was worth whatever punishment awaited him. In the evening, he felt the heavy hand of an MP on his shoulder and was marched into the military police hut. The officer on duty asked why that man had been arrested. The answer was: "Look at him, no necktie." Only then did the lieutenant notice the swastikas on the buttons of the man's shirt.

Pierre's slapped his knee and said, "It could happen."

We never had another chance to meet. Frequent transfers were the norm and we forgot to exchange addresses. *C'est la guerre....*

The directors of the USO decided to organize a bazaar for the men in uniform and called for volunteers. Gaming equipment was set up, local bakers donated their best brownies, test-your-skill contests were placed around the lobby, and further suggestions for activities were requested. If I could look like an American Indian, perhaps I could try another ethnicity? I offered to become a Romany for one evening and read palms. With the help of a library book, I familiarized myself with the names and supposed functions revealed by lines in our palms. I curled my hair, borrowed a long red skirt and an embroidered white shirt, and, with wrists tinkling with bracelets, sat down in my booth.

I had expected to enjoy this, the dress-up and compliments on my "gypsy looks." Everyone would surely know that I was a fake, not a true psychic. But, I was mistaken. Within the first half-hour, I realized many of my so-called clients thought me a genuine fortune teller. The line of soldiers waiting to hear what I might say about their future never stopped. Several men returned for a second session because they forgot to ask me something. They placed their hands in mine and smiled, but only with their lips. Their eyes betrayed their seriousness. Clearly, they needed to hear that their life-lines were long; that the little folds on the edge of the hand promised three or four children; and that they would come home safely from the war, be it Europe, Africa, or Asia. Once I understood their fears, I became uneasy. An interview might go like this:

"Hello, sergeant. My, you have a strong hand. Let's see what it reveals."

"Not too much trouble, I hope."

"This line tells me about a touchy family situation. Hmmm."

"Yes, that's my sister, acting up."

"There's a boy involved. But it will straighten out."

"That's a relief. The guy is a creep."

"I see health problems, not yours. I believe a grandparent."

"Yes, that's Grandma Bess. She's ailing."

Thus, the revelations of many of my clients created an aura of genuine second sight. Inevitably they asked about their life-line.

"It is long and unbroken. See how smoothly it crosses your palm? That indicates longevity, many long years."

Now, the smile reached his eyes. "I'll make it then. Through the war."

That should have been gratifying, but I suddenly I felt afraid. Should I continue this farce? I excused myself for a moment to consult with the director of the event. He assured me that giving hope could do no harm and perhaps could do good. I returned to my booth, but now it was my turn to smile when I wanted to cry. How many of these soldiers would not return? Over there, seated in the corner, the young man who had not spoken a word, probably no older than I, what was in store for him? And that back-slapping loudmouth, would he return to be a blessing to his family or would they gently rub his name on a headstone? Both were afraid but reacted in different ways. They had been called or they had chosen to fight evil beyond their comprehension. The only true second sight I experienced in my fortune-teller booth was my glimpse of the tragedy of war. Decades later, walking hand-in-hand with my veteran husband among the gravestones in Normandy, I learned from him that even those who came back with bodies intact were left with images and memories that time could not erase.

As my voice grew sore, I remained in my booth, angry with myself, gentler with my customers. How could I have forgotten this was not a party to entertain the entertainers? Silently and vehemently, I vowed I would try harder to look beyond myself and pay closer attention to the needs of others.

How poorly I kept that promise. Decades had to pass before I understood the depth of my blindness. Here I was, living in the Deep South, drinking from fountains marked WHITE, told to move to the front of the bus, and sitting comfortably at the food counter at the Five and Ten while black customers stood. I was blind to the separate drinking fountains, to the demeaning seating, to the segregation around me. There were no Negro instructors or students at the university, and I do not recall being served by an African-American in any capacity but a menial one, not in shops, offices, hospitals, or municipal facilities. On an intellectual level, I knew blacks were denied equality of education, health care, economic opportunities, housing, political rights, and much more. How was it possible that I, who had lived as an *Untermensch* in Nazi Germany, was so accepting of such inequities thriving among the magnolias?

My studies included courses in American History, and I did not ask why material titled "The Civil War" in Pine Bush became "The War Between the States" in Columbia. In high school, we learned the conflict was triggered by the expansion of slavery. In South Carolina, the issue was termed "states' rights." By whatever name, the struggle had been a tragedy and its aftermath a travesty, but I listened without challenging such widely different interpretations. The rather convenient rationalization that I was merely accepting the ethos of my environment will not do. I had lived, read, and studied enough to know human history is littered with justifications dressed in acceptable words. Perhaps my lack of indignation was due to the lack of personal contact with black people. They were there, but I did not really see them. My friends who were born in the South never spoke ill of blacks, they just accepted the status quo. But how could I have done the same?

Among the thousands of students that went to USC in the early 1940s, I had the privilege of quite literally sitting at the feet of a voice of righteousness. Dr. Morse was quite old and not well, but he was permitted to teach a class or two at his home. His field was sociology. We, the students, gathered on the floor of his living room while he lectured from his comfortable armchair. About halfway through the session, he asked us if anyone would object to visits from "colored" students from a nearby segregated college. No one objected. Then, Dr. Morse said:

"It would be best if you would kindly not discuss these visitors with anyone on the campus, indeed, not anywhere."

Three or four black students joined us for most of the remainder of the course. There were no firebrands among them, but their interest and intelligence were obvious. This was my opportunity to connect with these young men and women. But I did not try. Not until the leadership of Dr. Martin Luther King Jr. decades later did I acknowledge the presence of inequality as ugly sores on the American body politic. Like a doting mother, I hated to admit all was not well with my loved one, my America. It took time, but eventually I recognized genuine patriotism does not deny uncomfortable truths by mouthing platitudes, that love of country takes courage, the courage to speak out against injustices, especially those so beautifully burnished with the patina of tradition.

CHAPTER 9

THE BOYFRIEND

My bimonthly column published by the *Columbia Record* occasionally attracted complaints or plaudits from readers, neither of which I answered. But, I did respond to a complimentary note from a soldier stationed at Fort Jackson. Eli was from New York. He commented sensibly on my essay and asked if he might speak with me. I agreed to have him call. We talked a while, and he asked if he could take me to dinner—and that's how I met my first boyfriend. He was nice-looking, a recent graduate of NYU, the son of an Orthodox rabbi. He was an Army sergeant, and soon all our free time was spent together and we wrote letters between dates. He hoped to go to law school after his military service, and our conversations revealed many shared ideals. We laughed at the same nonsense, told each other secret thoughts, and thrilled at the touch of hands and lips. He seemed to support my goal to have a career. When possible, he came to hear me speak at the Elks or the Moose or the VFW. We were happy. He had a sister and, when I declared my determination not to sleep with anyone but my husband, I told him to picture his sister in a similar situation. That settled that. He gave me his college ring as a token of our engagement to be engaged. I wrote to my family, he wrote to his, and all was well in our private world.

One day, Eli announced his commanding officer would like to meet me. The middle-aged major was charming and, after the preliminaries, he asked me if I could be trusted to help with a small but pesky problem he hoped to resolve. My knowledge of German was essential, and I would never be in any danger. I managed to think "wow!" rather than say it aloud as I sat up tall. I knew US Army Intelligence was trying to determine who among the prisoners from the Afrika Korps housed in Fort Jackson should be sent home first once the war ended and who should be kept as long as possible. Behind the barbed wire a good deal of re-education was taking place, but it was almost impossible to know a prisoner's true ideology. The goal of creating a democratic Germany from the rubble would require men willing, perhaps eager, to participate in the process. I had mentioned to Eli that I might be helpful, if there was a way to let me mingle with the men. I had visions of myself as the secret agent serving the effort of our government to restructure Germany after the defeat of the Nazis. I asked the major:

"Do you want me to help figure out who among the POWs are Nazis?"

He shook his head and explained it would be most unwise to allow a young woman among German prisoners who had not spoken to a female for many months. He could not allow that. He explained:

"What I am asking you to consider has nothing to do with the Afrikaners. We have a case of a young soldier, excellent in every respect, and deserving of a promotion. He asks about it frequently, wants to know what he can do to get his corporal stripes. We have not given him an answer because there is a problem."

The major and Eli explained this private, let's call him Kurt, lost his wallet in the movies several months ago. The proprietor found it and sent it to his unit. From there, it landed on the major's desk. Why? It contained a letter, written in German, which referred to *Panzers* (tanks) and other military equipment. A background check revealed Kurt was of German heritage and, as a teenager, he had visited the parental fatherland. Since the discovery of the letter, Kurt had been under surveillance. That turned out a fruitless effort. The case needed to be closed. The question at hand: Was he a spy, a potential spy, or just foolish?

I asked for a copy of the incriminating letter. I slowly read it, twice. "How ridiculous is this?" I thought. But the two sets of eyes watching me were serious.

"Would you comment, please?"

"This is very badly written," I said, figuring this was my first and last moment as a secret agent. "There are many mistakes. No actual information is given. He tried to explain his Army routine: I got up, did this, saw that. The fact that it is addressed 'Dear Teacher' makes me wonder if this is a rough draft of some sort of school assignment. Perhaps he forgot that he still carried it around."

There were broad smiles from my fellow conspirators when I suggested they ask him, yes, just ask him what this was about.

The major replied: "Soon, not quite yet. Could you help us just a little more? Then, if you agree, we will confront him. We need more details about that alleged vacation in Germany. You will have to meet him—on a social level, someplace public. We can arrange that. A Sunday picnic of his unit on the lake will be a perfect venue. You'll come and we'll invite some other young ladies. You could chat, meet him, and later report to us. You won't see us, but we will know where you are every second."

I was familiar with the saying, "There were two ways to solve a problem, the easy way and the Army way." A picnic on a lake? For how many? How much would that cost? I wanted to shout: "Ask him, for crying out loud, talk to him." Instead, I nodded with proper earnestness while visions of Alice and the White Rabbit popped into my head.

According to plan, I gathered a few friends and we spread our blankets along the shore of the lake. A nod from the major identified Kurt. I introduced myself, and invited him to join me. He was friendly, but of course he would be—a girl had singled him out and there were probably fifty men there for every female. He was polite and altogether likeable. We ate, I asked him about his vacation in Germany, and we shared impressions of German vacation resorts. When I spoke German, he laughed, tried a few words, and gave up. After an hour, I decided to have a little fun. I suggested a boat ride on the lake. Kurt was delighted to take the oars. I waved my hand in the direction of the invisible Eli seated under tree and the major reading a newspaper in his Jeep. The water was cool and the company likeable as we enjoyed our turn around the lake. The image of two scowling faces on the shore inspired me sing the entire *Lorelei* in a voice rather too lusty considering the lyrics concern a drowning on the Rhine.

A few days later, I received a note of thanks with the news that Kurt was now a corporal. The mysterious letter in his wallet had been identified as part of an essay assigned when he tried and failed to enlist in the Reserve Officers Training Corps. He had forgotten all about it. End of story. Eli and I never spoke of the incident and I hope that after about seventy years my promise of silence is no longer binding.

I spent the summer following my first year at USC at our new home in New Jersey. My parents looked well; the winter had been long and restful. Freddy, though bitterly disappointed he couldn't join the military to fight the Nazis, had faced the reality of his limitations and found his first employment as ticket agent at the Passaic office of a New Jersey bus line. He used his spare time to perfect his English until he had not even a trace of an accent. He was taking courses in night school, which would, in time, allow him to become an accomplished bookkeeper. He visited our folks when he could. The German-Jewish newspaper *Der Aufbau* kept my parents informed and Mutti was, as always, a diligent correspondent. My father worked sun-up to sun-down and was proud of his growing bank account. The farm work was manageable, but even I could see the hills were too steep for the tractor. Papa had already fallen off and now he tied himself to the seat with a piece of rope. The purchase of a tractor specially adapted for slopes had to wait, it was too expensive. Perhaps in a year or two.

I was content to bask in the company of my parents. I helped Mutti with her chores. The Hollands paid me to clean their part of the house, and I served the meals when they had guests. It was wonderful to be the pampered only child, to be asked what I wanted for dinner, to watch the needle fly in Mutti's hands as she updated my clothes. The college world I had entered was unknown to them, but my parents were eager to share my experiences. Is there any satisfaction greater than the approval of the people you love the most? I think not.

My stomach felt calmer than it had in years. I read, and took long evening walks with Rexy, the invaluable shepherd-collie mix. For an animal lover such as I am, there was plenty of entertainment on this farm. Hanging around the kitchen door was Matschele, a black-faced lamb. Abandoned by its ewe at birth, he had been bottle fed by my mother. Although weaned and free to go as he pleased, the lamb opted for table scraps and handouts by the back steps. Attempts to have him join the small flock in the meadow failed. He simply stood by the fence and cried "baa-baa" most piteously. And then there was proud, aristocratic, full-of-himself Wulliwulli. His mother goose left her nest before all her offspring had emerged from their shells, and this gosling completed his incubation in a box on the kitchen stove. Papa was the first to lift him down and their bonding was permanent. When my father went down the lane to the local post office, Wulliwulli goose-stepped on his right, Rexy, with a swinging tail, was on his left. The two animals accompanied him regularly in his walks through the village, a threesome no one could view without a grin.

My favorite evening amusement was theatre in the barn. This, however, had no resemblance to summer stock. The farm was populated by over twenty cats, all colors, sizes, and temperaments. (Only one cat lived in the house.) At milking time, they assembled, lined up into shifting, switching, undulating rows, all eyes on my father seated on his milking stool. When he was ready, Papa would direct several streams of milk, warm from the udder, into the faces of the cats. Invariable, this was immediately followed by a grand communal wash-in. Flicking red tongues cleaned each other's fur, first with this partner, then selecting another, behind the ears, under the neck, around the eyes, no dummy don't show me your tail, turn around, ah, yes, that's yummy. No comic routine on stage or film has ever equaled that performance. When completed, a chorus of meowing signaled it was time to fill up their huge bowl with a third of a pail of milk. Papa complied. The jostling for the best place on the rim continued, bigger cats smacking the more aggressive kittens into proper etiquette while I gasped for air from so much laughing. Visitors who were treated to this spectacle wanted to know if the cats had names. Of course, they did: Mietzele. Which one was Mietzele? Papa answered, "All of them."

I returned to the farm upon completion of my second year of college, but during that summer I worked in a defense factory that was under contract with the government. My parents had met a neighbor whose job took him to Phillipsburg, a city on the New Jersey-Pennsylvania border. He was glad to have some company and help with the cost of gasoline. Rumors claimed the factory fabricated batteries, but no one was certain. Military secret, you know. I was one woman among rows upon rows who sat at long tables and manipulated little gray cardboard boxes with wires. The hardest task was not to fall asleep from the monotony of the work. The pay seemed wonderfully generous to me, as I earned enough to pay a year's tuition, my ticket back to Columbia, and something left for a new outfit.

Eli had been transferred out of Fort Jackson, but we arranged to meet each other's parents before I returned to the university. He came to the farm, where Mutti, Papa, and Freddy were charmed with my boyfriend. Then, it was my turn to meet his family in Brooklyn. I was excited and a little scared as I made my way by bus and train to the Ocean Parkway address. Thankfully, Eli had preceded me and surely would bridge any awkward moments. I wanted to like his family, but I never considered the possibility that they might not like me. From the moment I walked through the door, though, I stepped into enemy territory. The rabbi, in full beard, did not touch my extended hand—such religious orthodoxy was foreign to me. Eli's mother said very little. She spent most of her time getting the dinner on the table. But I did notice the way she looked at Eli: undiluted adoration. No girl would ever be good enough for him. Eli's sister was rather plain and a bit sullen. I would get no help from her. When the conversation turned to the Nazi persecution of Europe's Jews, the rabbi stated the assimilation of German Jewry was at the root of the abuse, it was God's punishment. I bristled. How could he say such a thing? Did he expect me to nod in silent agreement?

I could not allow such an accusation go by without a response. Trying not to show my anger, I countered that God had given man free will, that I rejected the concept of such a vengeful deity, and that the very notion of Hitler as an instrument of God's will was abhorrent to me. This did not endear me to the family around the dinner table. Eli said nothing.

During the twelve-hour trip back to Columbia, I tried to be fair and understand my chilly reception. Yes, I was poor, and surely their prize of a son could marry money. I was not reared to observe their rituals. I had argued with the head of the household, which was not acceptable. "Admit it, Rita," I thought, "you didn't come across as a suitable daughter-in-law." And Eli? He had not defended me, not even with a glance. I felt my stomach aching. The train, as always, was overheated, but I shivered during much of the journey.

By the time we rolled into South Carolina, my mood had changed yet again. Now I was furious. What did Eli's family expect? That I cover my hair with a kerchief or wear a wig and dress in long sleeves, even in summer? That I stay at home and cater to their son's every wish? They disapproved of me, so be it—I disapproved of them. But my greatest resentment was focused on Eli. I knew him to be an admirer of liberal Judaism. We ate non-kosher food in restaurants, he rode the bus to see me on Saturdays, and he had never mentioned attending religious services.

How, exactly, did he envision our future? Was it to be a life of pretense? Indeed, it was time for a serious talk.

During his next weekend furlough, Eli came to Columbia. Should I postpone a discussion that was bound to become difficult? I was tempted, but patience is not a virtue I could ever claim.

"Eli, after we marry, do we need to keep a kosher house?"

"Well, obviously. I want my family to be able to come and eat at my home. You can see that."

"Actually, until the visit to your family, I never gave it a thought. I'm not sure how I feel about that. Mostly I think it's hypocritical. What else would be expected of me by your family?"

"Just to join them for Friday night dinners and the Jewish holy days. Think of it a freedom from cooking."

"Really, not even a Seder with my folks?'

"Look, that's all in the future. I'm sure we can work it out."

I bit my tongue. After all, Eli was in the Army; he might be sent overseas any time. This was not the time to add to his worries. Also, wasn't it premature to discuss these issues now? Couldn't two people who loved one another find common ground? Though I tried, my mind would not stop creating scenarios of future controversy. Was it fair that I made all the concessions? I closed my eyes and tried to visualize myself five years down the road. There I was, dutifully following ancient religious precepts I rejected long ago, accepting my role as helpmate and as mother. My parents and Eli's would never be friends; the rabbi had shown me his disdain of assimilated German Jews. So, where would I stand? Right in the middle. The mere thought of my brother Walter debating God's death with the rabbi made me groan. Over the next several weeks my attitude changed many times. One day: "We will be fine." The next day: "Fine at what price?" I sighed and marveled at my Mutti and Papa; they cared only to see Eli and me happy together.

One evening at the USO I saw Henry, an army buddy of Eli's I had met several times. We chatted and then he said:

"Isn't that a shame about Eli's mother?"

"What are you talking about?"

"Sorry, but I was sure you knew. She had a nervous breakdown. Worried so much over her boy, she had to be hospitalized."

Eli had phoned earlier and not mentioned a word. He must have been troubled about his mother's health. But I could not muster much sympathy. I was too upset with him and with myself. Eli kept unwelcome news from me. That was unacceptable; I needed to be his partner, good, bad, indifferent—what mattered to one must matter to both. My disquiet about our future multiplied as I realized the poets were wrong, love it is not enough. Minds, too, must meet. My stomach hurt and my heart pounded in my chest. The best way to describe my ache was with a German word: I felt *zerbrochen*, imperfectly translated as broken into pieces, beyond repair.

When Eli called a few days later, I asked him about his mother. Eli hesitated for a moment, long enough for me to wonder if he was going to tell me the truth. He did. I then asked:

"Why did you keep this from me?"

"You are my darling, the bright star in my life. I will always tell you happy news, but why distress you with troubles?"

Wrong answer. I made an excuse and hung up quickly, not wanting him to hear me sob.

That evening, I sought comfort where I had always found it, in words. I took a notebook and began to record the story of our romance. How we met, the thrill of the first attraction, our walks with fingers touching, the first kiss, our discussions ranging from art to zebras, our inane hush-hush work in behalf of the almost-spy, meeting each other's families, and, finally, the cracks in the foundation of our relationship that crushed my dreams. Sorrowfully, I turned to a fresh page. "Dear Eli," I wrote, "I must return your ring. I sadly ask you to accept this difficult decision because, truly, we are not well-suited for one another."

For a week I revised the letter, revised my revisions, and finally could neither add nor subtract a word. I made one final copy into my notebook and put it aside for several days. Finally, I pulled out my best stationery and copied over my "Dear John" letter. It rained the day I walked to the mailbox and the raindrops mingled with the tears rolling down my face as I released the envelope from my hand.

Eli made several efforts to change my mind, but not once did he say that I was wrong in anything I had said.

Our relationship was over, but the letter had an unexpected life of its own. A group of students from the English and journalism departments published a monthly literary magazine. Occasionally, I contributed a short story or an essay. Walking across campus one day, the editor asked me if I had anything for the next issue.

"Maybe. I wrote a pretty good story in my creative writing class. It's in the cubby of my desk in my room. Take a look and use it if you like."

Several weeks later the printer delivered the new edition of the publication. Several students stopped to tell me how much they liked my story. I picked up a copy and gasped. The title over my byline was "Dear Eli: The Death of a Romance." I never told anyone that the editor had picked up the wrong piece—until now.

CHAPTER 10

MUTTI WROTE: 'TEACHERS NAMES CORRECT'

One day in the spring of 1945, my friend Ruthie received news that left her face-down on her bed, weeping in bursts of choking grief. Her roommate was packing a bag for her and calling a taxi to take her from the dormitory to the railroad station. Ruthie was going home; her parents had received the dreaded telegram, her brother had been killed in a battle on the Western Front. Just a few days earlier we had tried to console a fellow student who had been notified her fiancé was hospitalized, shrapnel had torn away his right heel. All of us wrote V-mail letters to soldiers, family members, friends, and GIs we had met at the university and the USO. The war overshadowed every other concern, nothing came close to its importance in our lives. We fell silent when we passed a house displaying the gold star that symbolized the loss of a dear one serving in the Armed Forces. We studied maps and leaned closer to the radio not to miss a word of Edward R. Morrow's reports. In 1944, the tide of war was turning. Germany was squeezed by a huge pincer movement, American and British soldiers closing in on Hitler's Thousand Year Reich from the west and Soviet armies from the east. Victory in Europe was in sight, and surely, Japan was nearing exhaustion. At long last, the phrase "after the war..." became a normal part of conversation.

Approximately 300,000 German and Austrian Jews had fled before the Nazi government initiated the "Final Solution," its euphemism for the mass murder of European Jewry. Families, such as mine, were horrified when news of the Holocaust began to slip through the filter erected by the State Department and other skeptics and cynics. Factories of murder run by Germans? Women and children? Even for those of us who had escaped, this was difficult to believe. But the evidence was piling up and forced us to accept the unthinkable. Could the relatives we left behind have been among the victims? What about my brother Jup? Oh, please, master of the universe, not my brother.... We had heard nothing from him since our brief reunion in Amsterdam in December of 1939.

Holland was liberated in April of 1945. For some months thereafter, mail service was uncertain. Of Holland's 140,000 Jews in 1940, 71 percent were murdered despite the Dutch people's hatred for their invaders and general empathy for Jewish suffering. Freddy appealed to the International Red Cross to search for our brother, but that humanitarian organization was overwhelmed with requests. A promise to post our inquiry on bulletin boards at centers where survivors assembled brought no results. So, we waited.

Toward the end of May, I was stunned to find a telegram in my university mailbox. With shaking fingers I opened it. The telegram had been sent by my parents. One brief line: "TEACHERS NAMES CORRECT. HAPPY MUTTI AND PAPA."

What did this mean? It had to be important because I had never known my folks to send a telegram to anyone. My friends were no help, they shook their heads as bewildered as I was. So, I went to find my mentor, Professor Wardlaw. He was as perplexed as I was. He asked:

"Your parents, they're okay? Not confused or anything like that?"

"No, they are perfectly sane. Do you think I should phone them?"

"It could take a while to get a call through and it's getting late. Perhaps you should wait until tomorrow."

I agreed, but slept little that night. In the morning, I hurried to the pay phone in the USC mail room. Before placing the call, I checked my box and there was a letter from my mother. I read it, then laughed and cried and ran all the way to Professor Wardlaw's office. He told me to sit down and breathe deeply. Then, I translated Mutti's German into English, sentence by sentence. She wrote:

My dearest daughter,

We have had such a strange week. I can hardly believe it, and I hope I can explain it properly to you. On Monday, we received a letter from Holland, one page, typed and signed "your loving son Jup." He said he survived the war and was most anxious to come to America. And then he asked us to send two thousand dollars so that he could make the necessary arrangements to join us.

At first your Papa and I were very happy, but after a while we were perplexed by the request for so much money. Also, it was so strange that he did not ask about his brothers or you. It just didn't sound like our Dicker. We wondered if he could have changed so much. Did he think we are rich? We read this letter over and over and waited for Friedel to come on Sunday to see what he thought. But then, on Friday, another letter arrived, also from Holland but with a different return address. This one was handwritten. The writer said he survived four years of hiding and fighting, and he hoped Rita, Friedel, Walter, and his Papa and Mutti were well. He said he has nothing but the well-worn clothes on his back, even his wallet had been stolen. If we could send him a few necessities, that would help and he would be very grateful.

When Friedel came, we made a plan. We sent telegrams to both letter-writers and asked them to name two of their childhood teachers. We even paid for their replies in advance.

Now we are waiting for answers. When they arrive, we will send one more telegram, this one for you, to let you know what happened. Papa and I and Friedel are tense and hopeful.

Your loving Mutti.

Professor Wardlaw and I sat grinning at one another and then he said: "I owe your folks an apology. They are more than just sane. They are very clever. Obviously, they expected you to receive this letter before the telegram. Such a simple—well, not exactly simple, but certainly wonderful —solution to the puzzle."

I splurged and called home. After laughing and crying, my mother confirmed that, as assumed, the second letter-writer identified Rektor Spieler and Georg Mai. There was no answer from the first correspondent. I asked for Jup's address, and later that day I went to the Five and Ten Cent Store in town. A large box in hand, I went up and down the aisles, stuffing the box with a pair of scissors; a knife, fork, and spoon; a shirt; some socks; a belt; needles and threads; bars of soap; a toothbrush and toothpaste; shaving cream and a razor; a small English dictionary; a pillow; a frying pan; and more. The lady behind the cash register looked rather perplexed at my collection, so I told her about Jup. She cleared some space and helped me pack and seal my carton. I lugged it to the post office and didn't blink at the expense of shipping it. Jup later told me how much he needed and valued my parcel. As for me, I never enjoyed a shopping spree as much.

How wonderful, indeed rare, that our immediate family, living on three continents, had survived. Years would pass before we all would sit around the same table once more, but, in due time, Jup and his Dutch bride made their home near my parents. He started his own landscaping business and some of the trees he planted in New Jersey still beautify the scenery.

As for me, I completed my work and graduated during the summer of 1945. Professor Wardlaw encouraged me to go to graduate school, and I applied to Columbia University, in New York. My request was denied.

My mentor was more upset than I was when I handed him the notice of rejection; he understood the meaning between the words while I did not. The letter from the admissions officer suggested I try again next year as the quota was filled for the present. I had experienced no overt anti-Semitism since coming to America, and I did not know that some universities limited the number of Jewish students they would accept. But, I was not particularly disappointed. It was time for me to support myself in the real world.

Professor Wardlaw asked me if my parents would come to my graduation. I said no, and explained the trip would have been too difficult and too costly for them. He asked:

"Are you upset that they can't be here?"

"Not really. I never expected them to come."

He patted my shoulder and said, "I'll come, not to replace your mother and father, but as your friend."

True to his word, he was there when I received my diploma and I was proud to accept his good wishes. The *Columbia Record* offered me a job on the paper and, although I was tempted, I declined. Mutti was not well, and Freddy was engaged to be married to a girl I had never met. Clearly, I must not put down my roots so far from my family; for their sake and for mine. It was time to look northward.

But, I did not wish to go home empty-handed. It had been my dream to repay my parents for their contribution of the cost of my college education. I often pictured Papa's surprise when I would hand him five, crisp, hundred dollar bills. What could I do to save such a princely sum in a short time? I had often visited with my friend Evelyn's family and had met her brother Jack. We had chatted amicably and, half-jokingly, he suggested I come and work for him after I graduate. Jack owned a successful business. Dozens of trucks crisscrossed several counties distributing beer and soft drinks bottled in his plant. Had he been serious? "Nothing to lose," I thought and called him. Our conversation was brief.

He promised to send a car for me when I was ready. I reminded him that I had no business qualifications.

"Don't worry. You're a smart girl. You'll learn."

The salary he offered seemed wonderfully generous and I was given the free use of a furnished apartment he owned. So, off I went, to a dot on the map of South Carolina, a dusty village of a few respectable-looking houses and many wooden shacks with outhouses in the back. Jack's bottling plant, warehouse, and twenty-some trucks comprised the only business; every working man and woman in the tiny community was employed by Jack, the Boss.

I settled into the three-bedroom apartment next to the office and found a stray kitten for company. I met the various managers and salesmen, but I still had no idea what I was supposed to do. By the time I figured that out, it was clear that I should leave. No, my boss had no sexual interest in me, I was not his type. He was a womanizer who preferred big-busted blondes and I did not fill such qualifications. I answered the phone and told callers Jack would or would not speak with them according to a wave of Jack's hand. I also was supposed to keep track of which truck was on what route and who was driving what and where, but I was not very good at that. The deep, Southern accent of the men as they pronounced the names of unfamiliar destinations often confused me. Most of my time was spent adding numbers, lots of numbers. Math had never been my strong point and I rarely got the same final answer twice. Jack was not disturbed by my poor performance. In fact, when he brought me papers to sign, I did not recognize my work. I asked what I was signing and he told me not to worry, just something about taxes. Eventually, I figured out I was attesting to the amount of money due federal and state governments on the sale of beer. Hmmm. The business had its own accountant, so why was my signature on these forms?

One of Jack's younger brothers had returned from the service and we enjoyed each other's company; neither of us liked lonely dinners. When I told him about the numbers game I was reluctantly playing, his response was, "Uh-oh," but he would not explain. My stomach began to feel sore. In four months, I had saved $500, and it was time to go home. Jack made no objection. In fact, he presented me with a first-class train ticket to New York. If I had any doubts that it was time to leave, they were dissolved in that moment. Clearly, I was way over my head in this environment. Lesson learned.

I spent a week or two at home. One day, Papa showed how much income tax he would be paying.

"That much?" I said, though it was quite a modest sum.

"Isn't it wonderful?" Papa said. "I can give something back to America!"

I found a job at a newspaper in Passaic, New Jersey, where my brother Freddy lived. Because my starting salary was very low, I was not able to pay rent even for a small apartment. The solution we found was practical and possibly unique: My employer had a friend who needed a female to sleep in his mother's house. The lady in question was visited by her children during the day, but was fearful to be alone at night. I became her unpaid, after-dark companion. We chatted in the evening, soon she prepared snacks for me and I had no problem sleeping on her somewhat lumpy couch. I renewed my friendship with Terry, my first roommate at the University of South Carolina. She had left after a year and now was recently married. Reuniting with Terry was one of the best things that ever happened to me. After all, no one ever did me a greater service than Terry. She introduced me to Leonard.

He was short, but I was shorter. Good: physically, we were a fit. He was good-looking, such clear blue eyes! We went to Coney Island and, after hot dogs and pizza from stands at the amusement park, my stomach hurt not from its usual anxiety, but from too much food. In the car on the way back to Terry's apartment, I literally turned myself upside down to feel better, head on the floor, feet on the seat. Leonard never blinked an eye, just wanted to know if that position helped me. Terry was sure after that performance Len would never call me. It was July of 1945. Len had been discharged from the Army just a few weeks earlier. He had just registered at St. John's University to finish his degree after the interruption of a tour of duty that included the Pacific theater of operation. He had started a job as well, but he didn't seem crazed with ambition. Len seemed like a man pleased to have done his service and pleased to be back home. Even on that first date, I liked this young man with the blond, wavy hair.

Despite Terry's concern, Len called me the next day.

The following day, he wrote me a letter. When could we meet again?

Just about a month later, Len took me to meet his parents. We walked into the kitchen hand in hand. His mother was up on a ladder looking for a platter for the roast beef. She greeted me with, "We'll have to fatten you up a bit," and she climbed down and hugged me. Len's father was not a hugger until he had grandchildren, but his smile was welcoming. This home was a comfortable place, not a waiting room before an examination.

Leonard spoke no German, and my parents had little English. But there are feelings that transcend languages. The day I introduced Len to my mother, Mutti pulled me aside. Her eyes on Len, Mutti cupped her hands and said to me, in whispered German, "He will carry you in the palms of his hands, he loves you so."

When it was time for Len's parents to meet mine, Mutti prepared a fine dinner and we ate on the porch of the farmhouse. It was a beautiful, fall day. My future in-laws had come to this country as toddlers, coincidentally on the same ship. Their backgrounds were in Russia, and they had used Yiddish in their parental homes. That was very helpful in establishing communication between our parents. It all seemed quite natural. My wedding was in a rabbi's living room and cost fifty dollars. It was mid-December, and we had about twenty relatives and Len's best friends, maybe 25 people in all. Terry's mother played "Here Comes the Bride," on the piano and after the ceremony we had wine and finger food.

How wonderful to fall in love and marry the right man, and to share fifty-seven years with him. We loved each other without either of us wishing to dominate the other, supported the other's career changes, never tired of each other's company, laughed and giggled into old age, and held hands until the day he died.

During those early days of our marriage Len attended night school. I was eager to study as well and earned my master's degree at Brooklyn College. It was almost impossible to find housing during the early post-war years, so we lived in rented rooms, a basement apartment, and then in a duplex owned by my in-laws. Eventually, we joined the exodus to the suburbs.

While still in Brooklyn I received an official, typed letter. Who could be writing to me? Margot and I regularly sent postcards across the United States. Walter's and my Airmails went over the ocean. But this was something different. I tore open the envelope and unfolded the typewritten piece of paper. Congratulations! My petition for US citizenship had been approved. I danced around the room and then settled down to read the instructions: I, and guests if I so chose, should appear at ten o'clock at the designated courthouse, answer a few questions on American history, and, if all went well, I would be sworn in as a citizen. Finally! I had hoped for this official acceptance for years and here it was in my hands. I could hardly wait.

On the appointed day, my husband, my in-laws, and a few neighbors invited by Leonard's mother arrived early. They occupied half of the chairs of the front row reserved for spectators. Future citizens were seated near the judicial bench. When my name was called. I stood. The questions were simple, and I answered them confidently. I smiled and sat down. But the judge was still looking at a folder on his desk. In a voice loud enough to reach every person in the room, he said:

"Young lady, I see here that you have a criminal record."

I was stunned. The murmuring voices grew still; everyone looked at me. I turned and saw the stricken faces in the front row. Len looked particularly confused—who, exactly, had he married? I was speechless.

The judge continued, but his stern demeanor was crumbling as he spoke: "I suppose you forgot, but on March 20th two years ago, in Columbia, South Carolina, you were cited," he was trying to stifle his laughter, "for jay walking! You paid your fine of two dollars." He began to laugh out loud. When he finally quieted his guffaws, the judge looked in my direction and said, "Sometimes, we just have to have a little fun."

My relief was quickly followed by anger, then a touch of the familiar stomach ache. The actual swearing-in ceremony was a blur. Len was sympathetic. Everyone else thought it was hilarious. I consoled myself, by hugging my beautiful, ready-for-framing citizenship paper and attached the stars-and-stripes pin to my lapel.

Both our children were born while we lived in Brooklyn, then we bought a house in Garden City, Long Island. I stayed home. This was no soul-searching decision; most middle-class women of my generation were busy with child-rearing and home-making. But, after seven years behind the sink, I had enough. When our youngest entered school, I wanted to return to the world outside my kitchen. Clearly, I had to match my work to the schedule of our children. That narrowed my choice to one —teaching. My master's in history should help my job hunt, I thought. I drew a red circle around Garden City to indicate how far I felt I should drive twice a day. Forty-five minutes or under, that was my goal. I called every high school superintendent within that circle and, after a couple of hours, was granted an interview. Thus began a career now stretching over fifty-five years.

I stepped into my first classroom without a day of teacher training. After a bumpy start, I discovered I loved the work. I learned something every day from my students. Eventually, to be certified, I had to take education courses; I found them useless.

My parents, in the meantime had moved to Passaic, New Jersey. Papa had fallen off the tractor once too often to continue farming. They bought a two-family house and when Jup and Nellie arrived from Holland, the younger couple moved into the ground floor apartment. Papa started a landscaping business. The first few weeks he simply rang doorbells and pointed to his tools. He cut hedges and weeded flower beds. Despite the fact that he knew very little English, Papa gradually created a successful business. Indeed, he eventually brought the son of his gardener from Winzig over to Passaic to work for him.

When the war ended, both the Steinhardt and Moses families remembered the Winzigers who had remained decent throughout the Hitler years. Many packages from Passaic and Minneapolis were gratefully received by former neighbors. One day, Papa asked me if I knew anyone who had a black tuxedo. In response to my bafflement, he added:

"No, no, not for me. Hugo Kliem wrote and asked if I could send him one."

"But, Papa, I thought they were really poor now, so what would he do with a tuxedo?"

"He didn't tell me, but I know. He thinks he has not much time left, and when he dies and people will come to view him, he wants to look like the man of stature that he was."

Len's parents owned a men's clothing shop, so my father-in-law always wore the current fashion. A few months after his old tuxedo left Brooklyn in a box labeled with the Kliem address in Winzig, Hugo's son Fritz sent us a black-bordered card. Hugo Kliem had died peacefully. Fritz attached a note to the announcement: "Thank you for the suit. My father was so pleased to receive it. He looked as dignified as he had hoped."

The fate of the relatives we left behind in Germany was unknown to us for some forty years. When the full impact of Hitler's Holocaust became known, we had to assume they were dead, but we had no specific information. Decades after the fall of the Third Reich, on a visit to the Jewish museum in Berlin, I stopped before a huge tome cataloging the names of Berliners killed in Auschwitz. Although I did not expect to find familiar names, I scanned the pages. I was about to close the book when a name caught my eye: "Eduard Markus and wife." He was my cousin,

Aunt Augusta's son. He was Edu to us, still in his twenties when we emigrated. We knew he had a girlfriend, apparently they married and were murdered on the same day. Edu had contracted polio as a boy, which left him lame and, although he was by no means disabled, no country would accept him. Walter had been his special friend and, after the war, had tried to find him. "Presumed dead," the authorities had informed him.

Walter had made his permanent home in England after the British government allowed the "enemy aliens" to return. He was in London during the Blitz, serving as a fire warden His own lodgings were destroyed by bombs. Nevertheless, he loved England, eventually found work in a dental lab, and married a lovely Englishwoman, Joy. To honor Eduard Markus' memory, they named their first child Mark.

Like me, Walter was quite sentimental about his childhood in Winzig. He always knew the words "German" and "Nazi" are not interchangeable. During his search for old friends, he found several former schoolmates, anti-Nazis who, along with their guilty countrymen, inherited the Nazi legacy of ruin, disgrace, despair, and a world that mourned fifty to sixty million victims of Hitler's war. Walter's efforts brought him into contact with Helena Guenzel Baumgarten, a love interest from his teens. She was the daughter of Winzig's chief forester, a man so highly respected that even Mayor Lang feared to harm him. My brother asked his once-upon-a-time sweetheart if she had any knowledge about the fate of our relatives: Uncle Adolph Steinhardt, his wife Trudi, Aunt Augusta Markus, and Herr Arnholz. Her response was an electrifying, "Yes!" Her father had played an important role during their final years and had risked his own life in a valiant attempt to save them. This is a summary of Helena's letters concerning the remnant of Winzig's Jews:

> My father was in charge of many hundreds of acres of dense forest. Somewhere among the oak trees was a small hut, probably used by hunters long ago. It was so well hidden almost no one knew of its existence. *Vati* [father] decided that it would make a perfect hiding place for Winzig's Jews. He would have known that

they had been ousted from the Steinhardt's house and were now homeless. I think that happened in 1942 or '43. We had heard the rumors about the terrible fate that awaited them under the guise of resettlement in Poland. I have no information how my father managed to offer these desperate people a place of safety, but I do know that they accepted. So they moved in, no doubt in the middle of the night. My mother had cleaned the place as best she could, but it was quite primitive, no electricity, no running water or sewer, and quite small for four people. As far as the town folks knew, the Jews just disappeared; those who cared did not dare to ask where they went. For about two years, they lived in the woods under harsh but habitable conditions. They collected firewood for warmth, my father brought them rabbits and an occasional deer he had shot; mother helped with home-grown vegetables and whatever they could spare from their own rationed provisions.

Then, just a few months before the end of the war, someone betrayed them. We never found out who it was. The two men and two women, all in their seventies, were ordered to appear at the railway station for *the* infamous "resettlement."

For many weeks, we feared that Vati would be arrested. He avoided going to town and, were it not for my ailing mother, might have fled; harboring Jews was a capital crime. I thought God must have protected him, but now I have my own theory why he was spared: Vati knew a terrible, truly terrible, secret. If he were arrested, he would shout it from the rooftops and that would enrage the townspeople and heap shame on the authorities. You surely remember Winzig's Catholic Hospital; the back of your garden was just across the lane. Earlier in the war, it had been converted to take care of patients with tuberculosis. These invalids had been moved from various sanatoria because now those facilities were requisitioned by the army for their wounded. The nuns, both quite elderly, stayed on and continued to care for the new arrivals. But, when the Russians began to counterattack, our casualties became enormous and more beds were needed.

One night, a large van pulled up in the back of the hospital. An SS officer explained to the sisters that new orders had been issued.

All the patients were to be moved to another, safer facility, farther from the Eastern Front. The Blackshirts were in a hurry to make the transfer, even helped to carry the stretchers onto the truck. The nuns were permitted to stay with their patients to help get them settled in their new facility.

But, there was no relocation. The vehicle stopped in the forest, as deep in the forest as the narrow roads allowed. Those SS bastards dumped dozens of helpless people on the ground and machine-gunned the lot, including the nuns. Then these true *Untermenschen* threw them into a ditch, covered them with some earth, and left.

When I picture that scene, I break out in a sweat, I am so angry and so ashamed. That's how they made room for more wounded soldiers. The murderers thought no one would ever know, but I think that Vati knew. Nothing in his forest could escape his awareness. That, I believe, protected him. He knew where the bodies were buried. Eventually, after the war, all the Winzigers learned the truth but I cannot tell you if the murdering troopers were ever tried for this crime.

By an astonishing turn of events, decades later, I, too, became privy to an additional glimpse into the last days of Winzig's Jews.

Sometime in 1965, the postman delivered a package to our house in Garden City. I was puzzled when I read the address of the sender. Why in the world would Herbert Schilk, a schoolmate from Winzig, mail me a parcel? The Schilk family had been among the Winzigers who never joined the Nazi Party and showed their good will toward us in many ways. Herbert never stopped greeting Margot and me when other schoolmates ignored or harassed us. His parents had rented the second floor of their beautiful house to Herr and Frau Arnholtz despite pressure from Mayor Lang to evict them. Once, Mutti sent me on an errand to Frau Arnholtz. Herbert saw me and he invited me to play a game of chess with him. I remember this clearly because it was so unusual to be treated with friendliness by a schoolmate.

Many years later, the Schilks were among the former Winzigers with whom I reconnected. After the death of his parents, Herbert and I corresponded from time to time. But I was puzzled to receive a package from him. When I unwrapped the box, I was completely baffled. What was this thing? This wooden tube, about five inches long with a wooden stopper? Then, I found the letter and I paraphrase and translate:

> You must wonder, dear Rita, why I am sending you the enclosed object. I am moving soon and when I went through my belongings I found it in a trunk we had brought from Winzig. My parents had told me that it was given to them by your Uncle Adolph Steinhardt. He had surprised my folks when he knocked on their door one night. This was during the winter of 1944. I was away then, in the army, and did not see him. My parents were very glad to see him, as he had disappeared so suddenly many months before. He did not explain where he had been and they did not ask. Your uncle said he had come to say goodbye, he had been ordered to report to the railroad station the following morning and had no expectation of returning from wherever he was sent. He said that he burned what few possessions he still had, but, somehow, he could not throw this one memento of his past into the fire. Then, he handed my father a small box and left. We kept it all these years but I believe it should be in the possession of a member of the Steinhardt family. So, here it is.

I held the tube in my hand, trying to figure out what its possible purpose might have been, but nothing came to mind. Nor did anyone else have any idea. Len asked me what kind of a man my uncle had been. I mentioned he had been proud of his military service for the German Kaiser. That was a clue. We began to research the gear provided to soldiers during the Great War. And there it was, pictured among the equipment issued to the German infantry. I was heir to a salt container, distributed along the western front of the First World War to prevent heat stroke during the summer.

Solving that mystery merely created a new one. Why would a man, facing the certainty of death at the hands of his countrymen, find it impossible to discard a trivial piece of army equipment? Why, indeed, had he kept it for twenty-five years? I knew he had fought in the war, but I had never asked him what rank he had achieved. In 1944, he certainly knew that Nazi ideology claimed that by nature Jews were incapable of patriotism. Perhaps a psychiatrist could understand my uncle's inability to throw away this symbol of his military service to a country that had turned against him.

CHAPTER 11

IRENE SAID: 'IT IS YOUR FORGIVENESS I NEED'

During my twenty years of teaching at Herricks High School in New Hyde Park, New York, I helped prepare many student-teachers from St. John's University in Manhattan. My reward was one free graduate course for each student. I took advantage of that offer during the summers. I enjoyed the sedate atmosphere and my unique status as the only lay person in the classroom. My compatriots were black-robed nuns and priests. One day, of my professors spoke to me after his lecture:

"Rita, you now have enough credits for a Ph.D. Write a thesis."

"Really?"

Len was enthusiastic: "Go for it." I had been thinking of recording the history of Winzig for some time, now the idea became the topic of my thesis. I worked seven years on completing it, traveled to Germany, passed the French language test, and the rather scary oral exam. After I received the PhD, a friend asked me how it felt to be a doctor. I said:

"Well, I still prefer to wash the kitchen floor on my hands and knees than to use a mop."

During the turbulent sixties, Len and I experienced the confusion and anxiety of most parents who tried to understand their teenagers. Sometimes, we felt changelings had moved into our house; the agreeable, friendly children, eager to share their days' events had been replaced by two strangers. Both our interlopers were activists, too. They marched the streets demanding the end of the Vietnam War; they regarded the government as the enemy; they trusted no one over thirty. They claimed to know how to create a better world, although neither had never held a job. They paraded rejection of their elders by their choice of music, hair styles, clothing, even their language.

So, I was especially delighted when, in 1966, my sixteen-year-old daughter, Ronnie, agreed to accompany me to Germany to attend a reunion of former Winzigers. It must be remembered that at the end of the Second World War, the Soviet Union had drawn a de facto boundary between Germany and Poland, known as the Oder/Neisse Line. At the Yalta conference in 1945, this concession was accepted by the major Allies. As a result, a third of the former state of Prussia was ceded to Poland. Some twelve million Germans, including Silesians, were ousted from their homeland. Many of these displaced persons settled in neighboring towns and villages in western Germany. Winzigers, like other displaced Germans, formed an organization that held yearly reunions with old friends from the hometown. The guiding spirit of these meetings was Winzig's former priest, Father Willinek.

The Father had contacted the bewildered refugees, most of whom had arrived penniless after a harrowing, disorganized, forced exodus, because he believed they would enjoy meeting again. As of this writing, these gatherings continue, now joined by members of the second and third generation. The Father established and maintained the connections first among his former congregants, and soon widened his circle to include all Winzigers. Without receiving any compensation, he founded and distributed his publication, called *Heimatklaenge* (Sounds of Home). His readers began to contribute articles and memories of their life at home, in Silesia. Nostalgia bonded former acquaintances and friends and they began to meet every year to spend several days' time in each other's company. The phenomenon of towns-in-exile spread and developed into a league with political as well as social agendas. The early hope of the league's members, to be permitted to return to their homes, was unrealistic in the post-war atmosphere. It is noteworthy that these displaced people, driven from their homes in mid-winter with nothing more than what they could carry, never advocated the use of force or terror to regain their territories. It also is remarkable, that, although the country was in ruins in 1945, the exiles were generally accepted and often helped by their new, western neighbors.

At the 1966 reunion, former neighbors warmly greeted the mother and daughter from America. Father Willinek was our host, and we stayed in his home for two days and nights. He drove us to the town of Meschede, where Winzigers were assembling. At the formal dinner, I was besieged with questions about my parents and brothers and the fate of the Moses relatives. In his address, Father Willinek expressed his hope that our presence implied forgiveness for crimes committed against us in the past. By this time, Irene had become a mere fragment of a half-forgotten childhood. But, after the meal, I spotted her in the back of the room. My first reaction was joy—there was my childhood friend!—and I walked, almost ran, toward her. But, in an instant, the familiar pain in my stomach brought back the other, the despicable Irene who had called me names and spat at me. I turned around and walked away.

Ronnie and I were staying at an inn that night. We were reliving the day's events when we were surprised by a knock on the door. I answered, and there stood Irene. Before I could shut her out, she said:

"I have waited a very long time for this moment. I must, I simply must, speak to you. If you don't let me come in, I'll stay right here in the hall all night and try again in the morning."

I stepped back and offered her the only chair, Ronnie and I sat on the bed. Irene spoke rapidly, with the intensity of someone overflowing with long-suppressed words. I paraphrase:

"My mother was the ambitious one. Father was content to be a mailman, but she decided to make him the postmaster of Winzig. She told my brother and me that if one hoped to get ahead in this new Germany, the whole family must be regarded as reliable Nazis. She joined the Party early, enrolled my father and told my brother Rudy and me that we must become members in our respective Nazi youth groups. My friendship with you and Margot had to end; she said it was an obstacle to father's promotion. First, she forbade me to play with you. I objected, I cried, she insisted. Next, she said father had a heart condition and if we children did not do as she told us, he was likely to have a heart attack. His mail pouch was too heavy for a sick man. Did we not love our Vati? How could we stand in the way of his promotion? Perhaps you remember, I was always afraid of her. And, so, I did all those things, those hurtful things, to you and Margot. I am sorry. For so many years, I have been sorry, sorry I did not stand up to her. Vati was made the postmaster and she was satisfied. She said we children had done well. But, I have not done well. I don't know how to be happy. Two divorces. No children. Later, I found out my father's heart was fine, she had lied. I don't know how to forgive that. But it is your forgiveness I need. Is it too late?"

What could I say? The room was quiet and then Irene whispered: "Please, Rita, remember: I too was a child."

Those simple words struck me like a blow. In all my fantasies, all those images of revenge and reconciliation, never had I thought of her as a child. Irene repeated:

"I need your forgiveness."

I reached for her hand, "You have it."

Irene wiped her eyes and I was grateful that she left quickly. Ronnie understood enough German to realize this had been an upsetting reunion, and now I translated the details for her. She hugged me and we fell asleep in the same bed.

Irene inadvertently showed me that Leonard and I needed to appreciate the way our children's bravado covered their confusion and anxieties. Together, we learned to respect their idealism, even though we refused to grant demands for irresponsible freedom. We remembered to argue with them less and hug them more. Now we know their generation was right to reject our "police actions" in the Far East. The end of the Vietnam War was largely their achievement.

The bond of love Leonard and I shared helped us to bear many losses: the death of parents, siblings, a grandchild, and the spouses of both our children. There were many funerals but there were also many births, weddings, and other celebrations. My mother was right years ago when she said Len would carry me in the palms of his hands, but I like to think we lovingly carried each other.

At this writing, my daughter and I live together and, even on those rare occasions when one gets annoyed with the other, nothing can shake the solid foundations of a loving relationship. I am 92 years old, still teaching, content with the knowledge that knowingly I have done no harm, and have done some good.

The stories you have read in this memoir are a thank you note to the United States. Indeed, I am an opportunist, certainly not a genius, not driven by grand career goals, never interested in accumulating wealth, but willing work my plot in the garden of this country.

Some sixty years ago, my brother Freddy and I met for dinner one night, just the two of us. We spoke of our childhood, laughed, and wiped a tear or two. Freddy reminded me of the day we stood together on the deck of the SS Pennland in December 1939 when we decided it was just too hard to be Jewish. We were going to convert to Christianity. And then, sitting comfortably in a restaurant in Passaic, New Jersey, my brother said:

"Isn't it wonderful? In America you don't have to."

And I said: "Amen to that."

Photos

Photo 1. Heymann Steinhardt, the author's father, c.1911.

Photo 2. Rosa Steinhardt, née Moses, the author's mother, c.1911.

Photo 3. The author's father during World War One, 1916.

Photo 4. The author's mother with sons Walter, Josef, and Siegfried, c. 1922.

Photo 5. The author on her first birthday, 1924.

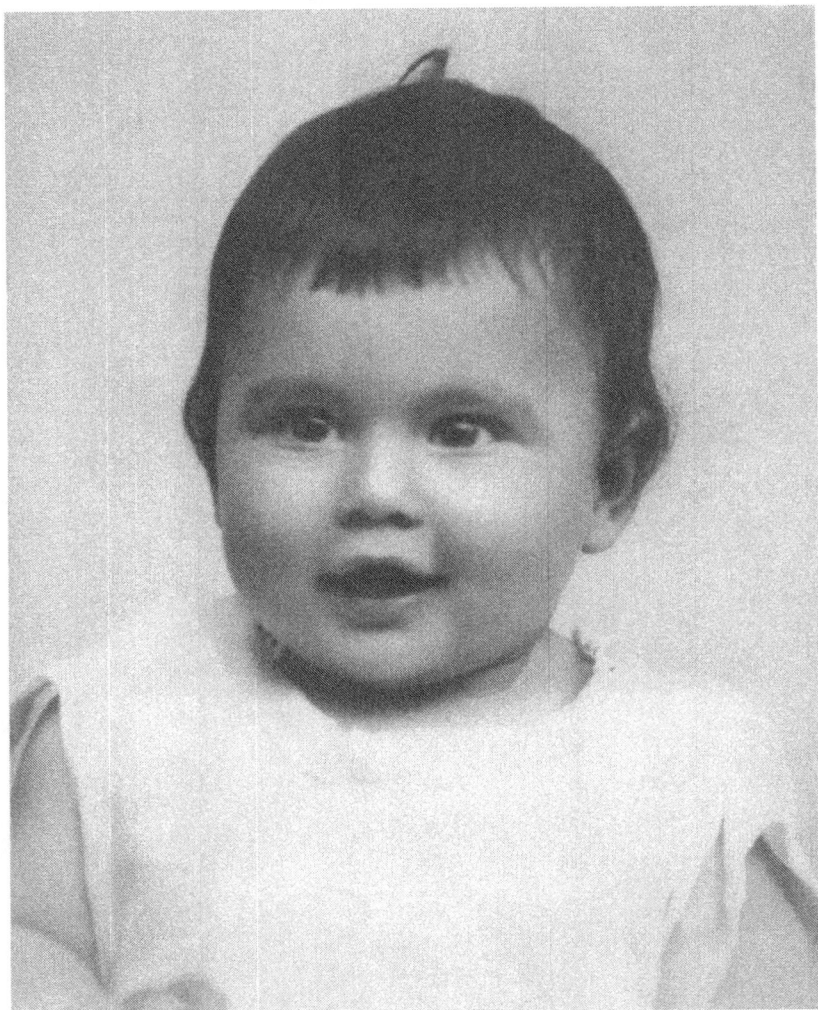

Photo 6. The first day of school for cousins Margot and Rita (the author).

Photo 7. The four Steinhardt siblings, 1933.

Photo 8. The author's parents in 1937.

Photo 9. The author's Nazi-required Identification card, 1938.

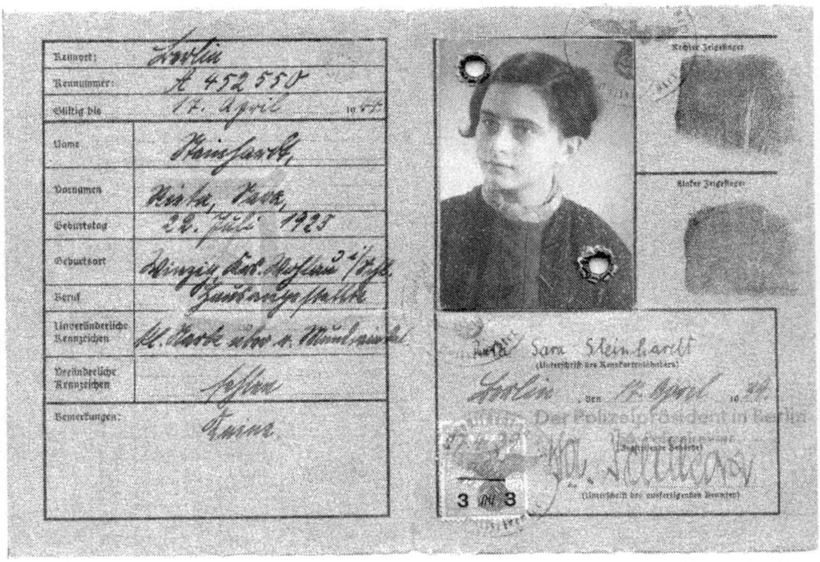

Photo 10. The author at the University of South Carolina, 1943.

Photo 11. Byline picture of author working at *the Columbia Record,* 1944.

www.ingramcontent.com/pod-product-compliance
Lightning Source LLC
Chambersburg PA
CBHW031301090426
42742CB00007B/544